A Balanced & Effective Prayer Life

Isaiah 56:7, Matthew 21:13
**"And said unto them, It is written, My house shall be
called the house of prayer."**

Matthew 6:7
**"But when ye pray, use not vain repetitions, as the
heathen do: for they think that they shall be
heard for their much speaking."**

1 Corinthians 14:15
**"I will pray in the spirit and I will pray with the
understanding."**

James 5:16
**"The effectual fervent prayer of a righteous man
availeth much."**

J. A. Twentier

Trafford
PUBLISHING www.trafford.com
North America & international
toll-free: 1 888 232 4444 (USA & Canada)
fax: 812 355 4082

Unless otherwise identified, Scripture quotations are from the King James Version. Scriptures included from other Bible versions are indicated as follows:

KJV King James Version
Scripture taken from The Holy Bible, King James Version. Cambridge Edition: 1769; King James Bible Online, 2017. www.kingjamesbibleonline.org.

AMP Amplified Bible
Scripture taken from the Amplified Bible (AMP), Copyright © 2015 by The Lockman Foundation, La Habra, CA 90631. All rights reserved

ASV American Standard Version
Scripture taken from The Holy Bible, American Standard Version (ASV), Public Domain

GNT Good News Translation
Scripture taken from The Holy Bible, American Standard Version (ASV), Public Domain

MOF Moffat Translation
Scripture taken from The Bible: James Moffatt Translation by James A R Moffatt, Kregel Publications, All rights reserved

MSG The Message
Scripture taken from The Message. Copyright © 1993, 1994, 1995, 1996, 2000, 2001, 2002. Used by permission of NavPress Publishing Group.

Please note that the emphasis within Scripture is the author's own.

Contents

Preface...9

Purpose and Scope...11

Dedication..13

Acknowledgements...15

I. A Balanced and Effective Prayer Life..........17

1. Three Basic Parts of Prayer........................19
   1.1 Relationship Prayer (upward focus).....................26
   1.2 Transformation Prayer   (inward focus) 32
   1.3 Dominion Prayer (outward focus)......................39

2. Praying in the Spirit and Praying with the
   Understanding...45

II. Focused Prayer 55

1. Prayer Agendas 57
   1.1 Pastor's Prayer Agenda (for the church)................ 63
   1.2 Church Service Prayer Agenda 65

2. Our Children -- Our Most Valuable Treasure........67
   2.1 Praying for Our Children...............................69
   2.2 Teaching Our Children to Pray.........................75
       2.2.1 Children in the Critical Decade (ages 16–26)................ 77
       2.2.2 Children in the Adolescent Years (ages 11–15)............. 79
       2.2.3 Children in the Formative Years (ages 1–10)................ 81

3. Driving Force for Fervent and Effective Prayer......85
   3.1 Our Burdens 87
   3.2 Burden for Others 90
   3.3 Burden of the Lord.................................. 93

Contents

III. The Vital Importance of Prayer 99

1. Prayer Tunes Our Spiritual Ear to Hear and
   Understand God's Voice................................101

2. God Works Through Man to Perform His Will
   on Earth..127

3. When the Answer to Prayer is "No" or "Wait"....153

   3.1 The Implications of God's Foreknowledge 153

   3.2 Why Prayers May be Denied or Delayed..................159

   3.2.1 No Human Reasoning for Unanswered Prayers 163
   3.2.2 Trial and Testing Develops Christian Character..................164
   3.2.3 Faith and Deliverance Vs. Faith Without Deliverance 170
   3.2.4 Twelve Apostles' Final Testimony Written in Blood................. 173
   3.2.5 Revelation of God to Unbelievers Through Miracles 175
   3.2.6 Answers Delayed Because of Sin 179
   3.2.7 Trials Become Testimonies to Others............................ 181
   3.2.8 Sickness Unto Death -- Promotion to a Better World.............. 181

4. Prayer -- The Last Frontier of a Mature
   Christian...183

5. Conclusion 193

   5.1 The Challenge.. 193
   5.2 The Answer to the Challenge 197
   5.3 Jesus' Only Prayer Request 199

6. My Prayer 211

6

Contents

IV. Appendices...**217**

Appendix 1 -- Prayer Scriptures...........................219

Appendix 2 -- Additional Books from the Author 227

Appendix 3 -- Notes......................................235

Appendix 4 -- Misconcepions Regarding Prayer.....239

Appendix 5 -- Prayer Ministry Tools 247

    5.1 Anonymous and Confidential Prayer Survey 247

    5.2 Faith Promise Prayer Pledge and Offering Cards 248

Appendix 6 -- Parenting and Prayer Notes............251

Appendix 7 -- Children's Prayer: The Forgotten
      Super Weapon of the Church 267

Appendix 8 -- About the Author.......................271

Preface

In my research, study and writing of the eight book progressive series entitled, "**I Must Be About My Father's Business**", I came to understand that the spiritual growth and maturity of a Christian revolves around three foundational processes or themes: **relationship, transformation,** and **dominion.**

From this understanding, I felt God impressed me to write a thesis dealing with the concept that a balanced and effective prayer life will include these three foundational building blocks or "A, B, C's" of prayer:

   (A) Relationship Prayer (upward focus).

      (B) Transformation Prayer (inward focus).

      (C) Dominion Prayer (outward focus).

Although there are other types of prayer, they will fit into one of these three categories. For example:

- Relationship prayer will include: thanksgiving, praise and worship, personal petitions for God to help you, etc.
- Transformation prayer will include: repentance, asking God to change us to be more like Him, etc.
- Dominion prayer will include: intercessory and spiritual warfare prayer (praying for the needs of others), etc.

A single time of devotion may not include all three parts of prayer, however, over time, a balanced prayer life will incorporate these.

The benefits of a family altar and family devotion in a home cannot be overemphasized. There is a small window of opportunity, that we have as parents, at each stage of our children's lives, to teach them and nurture them in the ways of God. And there is nothing more essential or of eternal value than investing in our children by praying for them and teaching them to pray. Helping them establish a connection with God in prayer will provide them an anchor that will stabilize and sustain them for the rest of their life; and assure their eternal life.

One of the greatest challenges of parents and the church is to place equal value and emphasis on teaching children and new converts to pray, as we do teaching them the Word of God. Both are equally important; however, God's Word alone produces information. This is the reason there are hundreds of religions that claim the Bible as the basis for their beliefs. But when God's Word is illuminated by the Spirit, through prayer, it will produce understanding and revelation. Revelation will affirm truth and create transformation in the life of a believer.

The first edition of this book is a work in progress and is by no means a complete exegesis on the subject. I would describe it as a beginner's guide for prayer (Prayer 101 – why and how we should pray). It is a summary of what God has dealt with me regarding this important subject. These concepts have helped me in my personal prayer life. It is my thesis and collection of findings at this point in my Christian experience. I understand that there is a risk in addressing this difficult and intimidating subject which is a "sacred cow" to some. But I also know, from experience, that the regret of not following your heart is far worse than the risk of criticism or being misunderstood in pursing something difficult or challenging.

The fact that you are holding this book is a testament to your desire to pray more balanced and effective prayers. May God bless and multiply your efforts in the Kingdom as you progress in your pursuit of a deeper life in the Spirit through prayer.

Purpose and Scope

The burden to write this book comes from a calling from God and is also driven by: (1) my personal struggle with effective prayer into my adult years; (2) my observation of all ages, in many different places, struggling with the same issues; (3) corroborating comments, regarding struggles in prayer, from men's ministry leaders, pastors, saints and other sources. The *"Forgotten Super Weapon of the Church"* in Appendix 7 documents the tragic results of not teaching children to pray and the overlooked power of children's prayer.

The primary purpose and scope of this book is to:

(1) Simplify prayer, for children and new converts, by defining its three elemental components. This is not done by describing lists of things to pray, but defining the three basic positions or focuses of prayer. Within these three foundational elements of prayer a description is provided for what may be included, but the individual's own words should be used.

(2) Provide a resource to parents praying for their children and teaching them to pray. Chapter 2, "Our Children – Our Most Valuable Treasure", deals with bringing prayer concepts down to the child's level, depending on their age (the A, B, C's of prayer).

(3) Help those struggling with prayer to develop a more consistent and effective prayer life.

(4) Provide a resource for teaching the simple basics of prayer in a Sunday school class or a prayer seminar in a church.

(5) Identify prayer as the key weapon over the spirit of the antichrist, which has exponentially risen in the world over the last few years. The evidence of this comprises a long list, three of which are: (1) the increase of atheist (40%) and agnostics

(60%) in the last seven years; (2) a great rise in antisemitism in the U.S. (17 Jewish centers threatened by terrorists last week), in Europe antisemitism is greater today than during the era of Nazi Germany, largely unreported by the press; (3) a lack of awareness regarding the fulfillment of endtime prophecy by many Christians and the resulting absence of urgency in the Father's business.

(6) Expose the lie of Satan, that we don't have time, in our fast-paced lives, to give God quality time in prayer and service. When we spend time in prayer and service, God will multiply our time by making us more productive in our daily activities and taking problems out of our lives that would cost us hundreds of hours. The following Scripture is generally used to support finances being given to God and the remainder being multiplied. But this also applies to the precious resource of our time which is more valuable than money: *"Bring ye all the tithes into the storehouse, and prove me now herewith, saith the Lord of hosts, if I will not open you the windows of heaven, and pour you out a blessing, that there shall not be room enough to receive it. And I will rebuke the devourer for your sakes, and he shall not destroy the fruits of your ground saith the Lord of hosts" (Mal. 3:10, 11).* Refer to Appendix 4, "Misconceptions Regarding Prayer" for additional Scriptures regarding this concept.

P.S. This book and the eight books in the series, "I Must Be About My Father's Business", are a product of hearing several thousand sermons, studying the greatest Book, the Bible, and other sources of great writers over the past 50 years. I have tried to give proper credit to sources. If I have overlooked someone or something, it is unintentional and only an indication that their individual work has blended into the larger themes of this 12 year, 12,000 hour, 2,500 published page project. Your comments regarding changes to the content of these books will be considered for future revisions.

Dedication

This book is dedicated to those who most influenced my life with their teaching and example of prayer:

Mom and Dad

To Mom and Dad, thank you for making some important choices in your life to follow and pursue God and His plan with all your heart. Thanks for teaching and exampling for me the importance of prayer.

Rev. A. H. Browning

To Rev. A. H. Browning, thank you for bringing the apostolic message to a small town in West Texas over seventy years ago. Under your great ministry and leadership our family was converted, discipled and learned the value of prayer.

Bishop James L. Kilgore

To Bishop James L. Kilgore, whose ministry, influence and encouragement supported and challenged and guided me for five decades. Your example and emphasis regarding the importance of prayer still impacts my life today.

These dear people have passed from this life, but I can still feel the effects of their prayers today. The lips that utter a sincere prayer may be closed in death and the heart that felt them may have ceased to beat, but their prayers are stored in golden vials and live on in heaven until the end of time: *"The four and twenty elders fell down before the throne, every one of them having harps and golden vials of incense which are the prayers of the saints" (Rev. 5:8).*

Acknowledgments

To my wife, Marsha Gail, thank you for 50 years of support and believing in me. Thank you for your encouragement, your editing work, and constructive suggestions in this endeavor. You are a great blessing to this project and to my life.

I would also like to say a heartfelt "thank you" to all my brothers and sisters in the family of God who offered their support and encouragement.

"The effectual fervent prayer of a righteous man availeth much." (James 5:16)

* * * * *

"To be a Christian without prayer is no more possible than to be alive without breathing." (Martin Luther)

* * * * *

"Prayer does not change God, but it changes him who prays." (Soren Kierkegaard)

* * * * *

"Prayer is the key of the morning and the bolt of the evening." Mahatma Gandhi

I
A Balanced and Effective Prayer Life

1. Three Basic Parts of Prayer

Every living thing (man, animal and plant life) is defined and sustained by three functions: **input, process and output.** Likewise, the spiritual growth and maturity of a Christian revolves around these three processes or themes redefined as: **Relationship, Transformation and Dominion.**

Relationship (upward focus) involves God and man sharing a mutual interaction of love, communication and trust.

Transformation (inward focus) denotes continuous change. It involves dying to self and allowing God more control of my life: less of my will and more of His will, less of my mind and more of His mind, less of my limited human love and more of His perfect agape love: *"He must increase and I must decrease."*

Dominion (outward focus) concerns God sharing His authority and power with man, as a son of God, to fulfill His will and work on earth as he is directed and driven by God's perfect love. This includes engagement in the harvest field and battlefield with dominion and authority over Satan and sickness – meeting people's needs of healing, deliverance and salvation.

Every concept in the Bible that pertains to Christian living and service relates to one or more of these three key subjects or themes. These three inter-related biblical concepts should be repeated in a continuous cycle to bring spiritual maturity and fulfillment of God's purpose and will for our lives.

Chart P-1

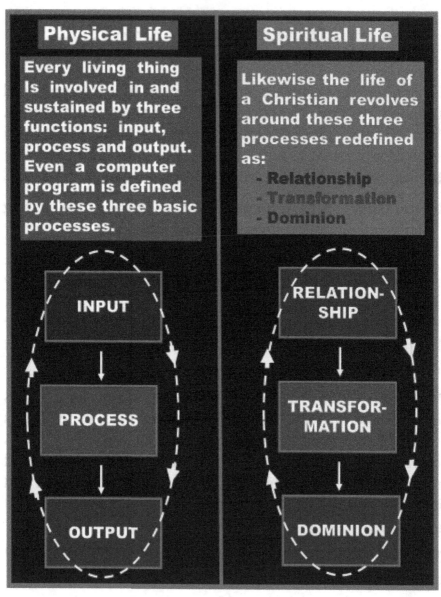

Three Positions or Focuses of Prayer
(Upward, Inward and Outward)

A balanced and effective prayer life will include:
- **Relationship Prayer** (upward focus).
- **Transformation Prayer** (inward focus).
- **Dominion Prayer** (outward focus).

Although there are other types of prayer, however, they will fit into one of these three categories. Refer to PowerPoint Charts P-2, P-3, P-4 and P-5 on the following pages of this chapter.

Isaiah's Life-changing Vision and Prayer

Isaiah felt extremely secure under the leadership, friendship and protection of King Uzziah. But Isaiah's relationship with Jehovah God was not complete; because he was trusting too much in a powerful earthly king and not enough in the heavenly King. After King Uzziah's death, Isaiah stopped by the house of God. Isaiah's vision and rededication recorded in Isaiah, Chapter 6 describes his life-changing vision and encounter with God, and illustrates these three key elements and positions in prayer.

Upward vision: Isaiah saw the Lord in His power, glory and holiness. He saw his need to renew his **relationship** with God. It was a vision of height -- the Lord high and lifted up: *"I saw the Lord sitting upon a throne, high and lifted up, and his train filled the temple."* It was a vision of God's holiness: *"The seraphims crying to one another: Holy, holy, holy, is the Lord of hosts: the whole earth is full of his glory."*

Inward vision: He saw himself and his need for repentance, and **transformation**. It was a vision of depth. He saw the

21

recesses of his own heart that needed to be cleansed and changed. It was a vision of helplessness (my needs): *"Woe is me! for I am undone; because I am a man of unclean lips, and I dwell in the midst of a people of unclean lips."*

Any time we draw near to God and feel His awesome presence and holiness, we feel the need to fall at His feet in confession and repentance. And God's response will always be, like that to Isaiah: *"Thine iniquity is taken away, and thy sin purged."*

Outward vision: He saw the world and the needs of others. He heard the call to step into the **dominion** role to do God's will and work. It was a vision of breadth that revealed a world with needs that must be met. It was a vision that revealed the desire of God's heart -- for someone to deliver His message to the world. *"Whom shall I send, and who will go for us?"* (God's needs). And finally, it was Isaiah's response that we all must make: *"Then said I, Here am I; send me."*

Chart P-2

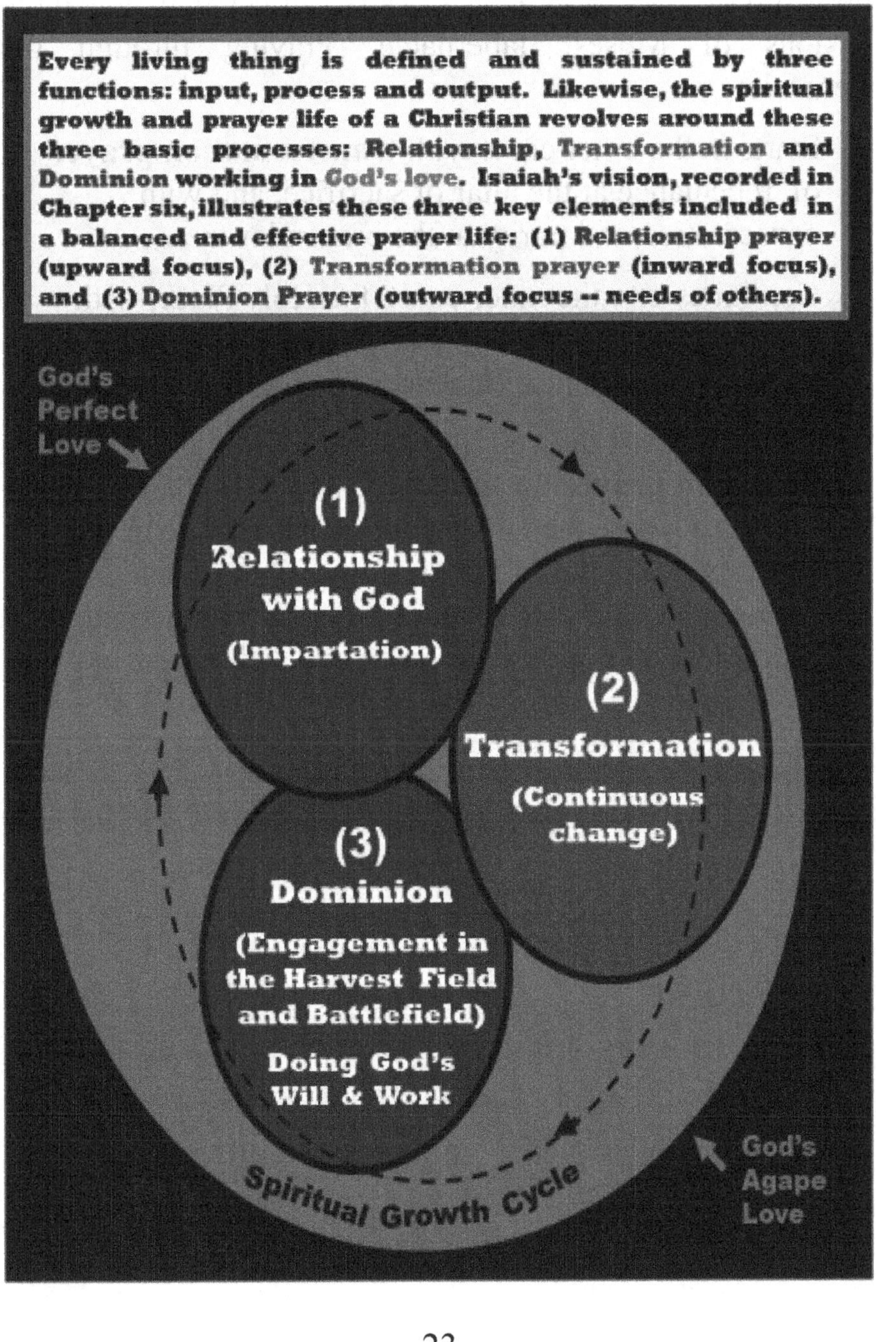

Every living thing is defined and sustained by three functions: input, process and output. Likewise, the spiritual growth and prayer life of a Christian revolves around these three basic processes: Relationship, Transformation and Dominion working in God's love. Isaiah's vision, recorded in Chapter six, illustrates these three key elements included in a balanced and effective prayer life: (1) Relationship prayer (upward focus), (2) Transformation prayer (inward focus), and (3) Dominion Prayer (outward focus -- needs of others).

God's
Perfect
Love

(1)
Relationship
with God
(Impartation)

(2)
Transformation
(Continuous change)

(3)
Dominion
(Engagement in the Harvest Field and Battlefield)
Doing God's Will & Work

Spiritual Growth Cycle

God's
Agape
Love

Moses' Tabernacle

These three types of prayer are also reflected in the three divisions of Moses' tabernacle. Praying through the tabernacle:

1. Starts in the outer court with **transformation prayer** of repentance at the altar of sacrifice, and with consecration and purity at the brazen laver.

2. Continues into the inner court, the Holy Place, with **relationship prayer** of thanksgiving, praise and worship at the altar of incense.

3. Continues past the veil into the Most Holy Place with **dominion prayer** that affect the needs of others. This is the place where the Gifts of the Spirit operate in the supernatural realm in partnership with our great omnipotent God. Here, there is access to supernatural power and dominion over Satan and sickness.

The descriptions of Relationship, Transformation and Dominion prayers on the following pages are provided as a basic guide or pattern for a balanced and effective prayer life.

However, your own words should be used in:

(1) **Relationship prayer**: thanking, praising, worshipping and making petitions to our wonderful heavenly Father – the King of kings and Lord of lords.

(2) **Transformation prayer**: confession, repentance and asking God to change us to be more like Him (less of me and more of Him).

(3) **Dominion prayer**: intercessory prayer and spiritual warfare prayer to impact our lost world; prayer for God's wisdom and direction in pursuing His will and work in the battlefield and harvest field.

The prayer Charts (P-3, P-4, P-5) may be printed and put on a prayer board or wall. Colored sticky notes may be used to add your own unique prayer request to each of these charts.

1.1 Relationship Prayer (upward focus)

Chart P-3

Relationship Prayer

- **Our focus is upward: adoration of our great God, making our petitions known and listening for His Voice.**

Thanksgiving:
Thanking God for His love and blessings:
- Spiritual Blessings (salvation, knowledge of truth)
- Relationship Blessings (family and friends)
- Physical Blessings (Resources He has graciously given us to manage):
  - Time (years of life)
  - Health (strength to enjoy life and do His will)
  - Wealth (finances and possessions)
- Protection from: harm, danger, sickness, and disease

"Enter into his gates with thanksgiving, and into his courts with praise be thankful unto him, and bless his name." (Ps. 100:4)

Praise & Worship:
Confessing who God is:
- His goodness: loving, forgiving, merciful, gracious, kind, faithful, long suffering, generous, burden bearer . . .
- His greatness: supernatural, omnipotent, omniscient, omnipresent, eternal, healer, ruler of the universe . . .

Petitions:
Request for my needs to be supplied: health, family, finances, careers, decisions, relationships, protection . . .

---

(1) Thanksgiving (for God's love and blessings)

Psalms 100:4, 5
*4 Enter into his gates with **thanksgiving**, and into his courts with **praise**: be **thankful** unto him, and bless his name.*
*5 For the Lord is **good**; his **mercy** is everlasting; and his truth endureth to all generations.*

This Scripture illustrates what God would have us do as we enter into His presence in prayer:
   - Thankfulness for His blessings and goodness.
   - Praise for His power and greatness.

Thanksgiving is an attitude of the heart. It requires a recollection or recalling of what God has done for us – His bountiful blessings.

   (a) Thanking God for **spiritual blessings:**
         - Dying in our place.
         - Bringing us to the knowledge of the truth.
         - Directing our steps.
         - The salvation experience.
         - The church and the fivefold ministry.
         - . . . .

   (b) Thanking God for **relationship blessings:** our spouse, children, grandchildren, extended family and the family of God.

   (c) Thanking God for **physical blessings:** the resources He has graciously given us to manage (investing first in God's Kingdom and then in our kingdom):
         - Time (the years of our life).
         - Health (strength to pursue life and God's will).

27

- Wealth (finances to meet our needs: food, clothing and shelter, possessions to enjoy).

(d) Thanking God for **blessings of protection** from harm and danger, sickness and disease, the evils and temptations of this world.

(e) . . . .

(2) Praise (acknowledges God's greatness and power)

In praising God we affirm and confess His greatness and use every wonderful attribute we can think of to describe Him:

- The prophet Isaiah states that: *"He is wonderful, counsellor, the mighty God, the everlasting Father and the Prince of Peace."*
- He is holy, kind, forgiving, gracious, merciful, loving, faithful, generous, longsuffering, awesome, peaceful, supernatural, . . .
- He is my refuge and fortress, my healer, my burden bearer and the lifter of my head.
- He is omnipotent (all powerful). He is omniscient (all knowing). He is omnipresent (everywhere). He can do anything and everything.

Throughout the Bible, the commands to "praise the Lord" are too numerous to reference here. Angels and the heavenly hosts are commanded to praise the Lord (Psalms 89:5; 103:20; 148:2). All inhabitants of the earth are instructed to praise the Lord (Psalms 138:4; Rom. 15:11). We can praise Him with singing (Isa. 12:5; Psalms 9:11), with shouting (Psalms 33:1; 98:4), with clapping (Psalms 47:1), with the dance (Psalms 150:44), and with musical instruments (1 Chron. 13:8; Psalms 108:2; 150:3-5).

God's response to thanksgiving and praise:

*"As the trumpeters and singers were as one, to make one sound to be heard in **praising and thanking** the LORD; and when they lifted up their voice with the trumpets and cymbals and instruments of musick, and praised the LORD, saying, For he is good; for his mercy endureth for ever: that then the house was filled with a cloud, even the house of the LORD; So that the priests could not stand to minister by reason of the cloud: for **the glory of the LORD had filled the house of God**"* (2 Chron. 5:13).

- **Thanksgiving and Praise is a cure for discouragement.**

(3) Worship (glorify and exalt God). Recognizing God's supremacy and authority in our life.

The dictionary defines worship as: "(1) Reverence offered a divine being or supernatural power (2) Extravagant respect or admiration for or devotion to an object of esteem (worship of God or an idol)."[1]

The Difference in Worship and Praise: Praise is universal and can be applied to other relationships as well. We can praise our family or friends. It is simply the truthful acknowledgment of the noble acts of another. Since God has done many wonderful deeds, He is worthy of praise (Psalms 18:3). However, **worship should be reserved for God alone:** *"Worship the Lord your God and only the Lord your God. Serve him with absolute single-heartedness" (Luke 4:8). MSG*

We must exalt God for who He is, not just for what He has done for us. To truly worship God, we must humble ourselves and surrender our lives to His control -- placing Him first above everyone and everything. Worship is a lifestyle, not just an occasional verbal activity. It is impossible to worship God and anything else at the same time: *"For it is written, Thou shalt worship the Lord thy God, and him only shalt thou serve" (Matt. 4:10).*

- **A good measure of our worship is the difference between how low we humble ourselves and how high we exalt our great God.**

Worship is an attitude of the heart. A person can go through the outward motions and not be worshipping: *"This people draweth nigh unto me with their mouth, and honoureth me with their lips; but their heart is far from me. But in vain they do worship me" (Matt. 15:8-9).* God sees the heart, and He desires and deserves sincere, heartfelt worship.

Two elements involved in being a true worshipper are Spirit and truth: *"But the hour cometh, and now is, when the true worshippers shall worship the Father in spirit and in truth: for the Father seeketh such to worship him. God is a Spirit: and they that worship him must worship him in spirit and in truth" (John 4:23, 24).*

Mankind was created to worship the Lord: *"Thou art worthy, O Lord, to receive glory and honour and power: for thou hast created all things, and for thy pleasure they are and were created" (Rev. 4:11).*

Jesus warned of the consequences of withholding worship: *"And he answered and said unto them, I tell you that, if these should hold their peace, the stones would immediately cry out" (Luke 19:40).*

- **More important than our words of worship are our actions of worship -- placing God first in our life. If anything has a higher priority, it is an idol and becomes the object of our worship.**

-- **From "A Look Into Your Heart"**

What could your idol be? Anything that you value more than God -- even though it may be good in itself -- for this takes His place in your life. Anything that you prefer to God, whom you are called to love above all else. Your work, your career -- no time for Him. Your reputation, your status -- no honor for Him. Your family, life, husband or child -- God does not have first place in your life. Your house, your home -- instead of treasure in heaven. Your vacations, your travels -- instead of time spent with God. Your health, your appearance. Every earthly thing that devalues for you the divine gifts received through fellowship with Him. Everything that is more important to you than the Lord.[2]

(4) Petitions (request for our needs)

This includes prayer and supplication to God for our own personal needs: health, family, personal relationships, careers, finances, decisions in life; protection from harm and danger, sickness and disease, the evils and temptations of Satan.

- **When we have taken our relationship prayer as far as we can with our human mind and understanding, we can then begin praying in the Spirit where the Spirit makes intercession for us.**

1.2 Transformation Prayer (inward focus)
Chart P-4

Transformation Prayer

- ## Our focus is inward: the need to be transformed -- continuously changed.

"Be ye transformed by the renewing of your <u>mind</u>, that you may prove what is the good and acceptable <u>will</u> of God." (Rom. 12:2)

"There are given unto us exceeding great and precious promises: that by these ye might be partakers of His divine nature." (2 Pet. 1:4)

Confession & Repentance:

- A plea for cleansing and forgiveness (Psalms 51)

- Repentance for any pride or self-righteousness

- Asking God to correct me with His written Word, preached Word, man of God, His still small Voice . . .

Transformation: (Change me prayers)

- Less of my will and more of His

- Less of my mind and ways and more of His

- Less of my limited love and more of His agape love

- Asking God to help me to identify and remove any hindrances to the flow of His love and power through my life

- Renewal of the Holy Ghost: "Building up yourselves on your most holy faith, praying in the Holy Ghost." (Jude 20)

He must increase and I must decrease !

(1) "Search Me and Change Me" Prayer:

Asking God to search me and identify any hindrances to the flow of His love and power through my life. *"Search me, O God, and know my heart: try me, and know my thoughts: And see if there be any wicked way in me, and lead me in the way everlasting" (Psalms 139:23, 24).* We should ask God to search our hearts and in areas where we do not have His favor, ask Him to correct us with His: written Word, the preached Word, a man of God, a vision or dream, His still small Voice, and even a trial.

(2) "Repentance of Sin" Prayer:

King David's sincere prayer of repentance is recorded in Psalms, Chapter 51. Notice that he says when he is forgiven and transformed and his relationship with God restored, he will once again fulfill his dominion role of ministering to the needs of others -- teaching and converting sinners. *"Have mercy upon me, O God, according to thy lovingkindness: according unto the multitude of thy tender mercies blot out my transgressions. Wash me thoroughly from mine iniquity, and cleanse me from my sin. Purge me with hyssop, and I shall be clean: wash me, and I shall be whiter than snow. Hide thy face from my sins, and blot out all mine iniquities. Create in me a clean heart, O God; and renew a right spirit within me. Cast me not away from thy presence; and take not thy holy spirit from me. Restore unto me the joy of thy salvation; and uphold me with thy free spirit. **Then will I teach transgressors thy ways; and sinners shall be converted unto thee**" (Psalms 51:1, 2, 7, 9-13).*

Although repentance includes sins of the flesh, early in our Christian walk we should gain dominion over the works of the flesh listed in Galatians 5:19-21.

Gal. 5:24
And those who belong to Christ Jesus (the Messiah) have crucified the flesh (the godless human nature) with its passions and appetites and desires. AMP

Rom. 6:14
For sin shall not [any longer] exert dominion over you, *since now you are not under Law [as slaves], but under grace [as subjects of God's favor and mercy]. AMP*

The greater lifetime struggle will be with the sins of **self -- the soul (the will, the mind and the emotions):**
  - Our will vs. God's will.
    - Our mind and ways vs. God's mind and ways.
      - Our human love vs. God's perfect agape love.

When apostle Paul states: "I die daily", he was not having trouble with sins of the flesh. He was having trouble with Paul – with self.

The only solution to the sins of self is to be crucified with Christ: *"I am crucified with Christ: nevertheless I live; yet not I, but Christ liveth in me: and the life which I now live in the flesh I live by the faith of the Son of God, who loved me, and gave himself for me"* (Gal. 2:20).

(3) "Repentance of Self" Prayer:

Repenting of the deadly sins of self (my will, mind and emotions). Emptying of self to be filled with more of God's Spirit – to be more effective working in His Kingdom.

- **Selfishness, self-righteousness, self-will and other self-centered traits are the greatest sins of the soul.**

   "**Selfish:** Obsessed with self, too much concerned with one's own welfare or interest vs. having concern for others." [1]

   "**Self-righteous (pride):** Filled with or showing a conviction of being morally superior, or more righteous than others; smugly virtuous. Being critical of others."[1]

The Spirit of God residing in our spirit affords us communion, comfort and peace. But the purpose of God's Spirit is to accomplish a much deeper work in our life. And that is for the transforming power of the Holy Ghost to change our will, mind and emotions to be like those of Christ.

Our prayer should be that we would be changed by God's transforming power:
   - Less of my will and more of His.
   - Less of my mind and ways and more of His.
   - Less of my human love and emotions and more of His love and compassion (enabling us to love our lost world, and even our enemies) with God's agape love.
   - Removing every trace of pride and self-righteousness and replacing it with true humility.

There must be a rending of the veil of self, which limits God's

35

access to our lives. This involves a lifetime process of change and transformation:

*"**Rend your heart, and not your garments, and turn unto the Lord your God**: Blow the trumpet in Zion, sanctify a fast, call a solemn assembly: Let the priests, the ministers of the Lord, weep between the porch and the altar" (Joel 2:13, 15, 17).*

"Then the Lord will answer: sending the rain . . . providing provision . . . restoring the years. . . and pouring out His Spirit on all flesh" (Joel 2:23-28).

The purpose of the Holy Ghost is to give us divine power to be transformed and take on His divine nature. Our prayer should be that the attributes of His divine nature would be added to our lives:

*"According as his **divine power** hath given unto us all things that pertain unto life and godliness . . . Whereby are given unto us exceeding great and precious promises: that by these ye might be partakers of the **divine nature**. . . And beside this, giving all diligence, add to your **faith** . . . **virtue** . . . **knowledge** . . . **temperance** . . . **patience** . . . **godliness** . . . **brotherly kindness** . . . **charity.** For if these things be in you, and abound, they make you that ye shall neither be barren nor unfruitful in the knowledge of our Lord Jesus Christ . . . **For if ye do these things, ye shall never fall** (2 Peter 1:3-8, 10).*

(4) Praying the Scriptures regarding continuous change and transformation:

	Dear God help me to:
Rom. 12:2	*Be ye transformed by the renewing of my **mind**, that I may prove what is that good, and acceptable, and perfect, **will of God**.*
Heb. 6:1	*Go on to perfection.*
Phil. 1:9	*Abound more and more in knowledge and discernment.*
Phil. 3:14	*Press toward the mark for the prize of the high calling in Christ Jesus.*
1 Cor. 9:25	*Strive for the mastery, and be temperate in all things.*
2 Peter 3:18	*Grow in the grace and knowledge of your Lord and Savior Jesus Christ.*
2 Cor. 4:16	*Experience a renewing of the inward man day by day.*
2 Cor. 3:18	*Be transformed into His likeness in an ever greater degree of glory. GNT*
Rom. 8:2	*Be conformed to the image of Christ.*

- **There must be death to self so that Christ can live His will through my life -- giving all of me to receive all of Him:** *"Except a corn of wheat fall into the ground and die, it abideth and die, it abideth alone: but if it die, it bringeth forth much fruit" (John 2:24).*

- **When we have taken our transformation prayer as far as we can with our human mind and understanding, we can then begin praying in the Spirit where the Spirit makes intercession for us.**

1.3 Dominion Prayer (outward focus)

Chart P-5

Dominion Prayer

- **Our focus is outward:** the need of people for healing and salvation.

Intercessory Prayer (friendly forces):

Standing between God and man, weeping and interceding for our lost neighbors, city, and world.

Spiritual Warfare (unfriendly forces):

Standing between Satan and man and binding the powers of evil that have bound and blinded them from coming to the light of the Gospel and the knowledge of Jesus Christ.

God's Direction and Wisdom:

Praying for God's wisdom and direction to know how to most effectively reach our lost world.

Praying Prophecies into Fulfillment:

Praying into fulfillment the promises and prophecies in God's Word regarding the complete restoration of the church with apostolic power and dominion over Satan and sickness.

"He called His twelve disciples together, and gave them power and authority over all devils and diseases." (Luke 9:1)

"The Lord appointed seventy also . . . heal the sick . . . I give you power over all the power of the enemy." (Luke 10:1-19)

Dominion means to dominate with authority and power, to rule in a territory or domain. This involves God sharing His authority and power with man in a partnership as a son of God to fulfill His purpose, doing His will and work on earth.

(1) **Intercessory Prayer** (friendly forces)

Standing between God and man; weeping and interceding for our lost neighbors, city and world.

Ezek. 9:4, 6
4 And the Lord said unto him, Go through the midst of the city, through the midst of Jerusalem, and set a mark upon the foreheads of the men that sigh and that cry for all the abominations that be done in the midst thereof.
6 Slay utterly old and young, both maids, and little children, and women: but come not near any man upon whom is the mark; and begin at my sanctuary. Then they began at the ancient men which were before the house.

1 Tim. 2:1, 3, 4
*1 I exhort therefore, that, first of all, supplications, prayers, **intercessions**, and giving of thanks, be made for all men;*
3 For this is good and acceptable in the sight of God our Saviour;
*4 Who will have **all men to be saved, and to come unto the knowledge of the truth**.*

Weeping like Jesus over our city: *"And when he was come near, he beheld the city, and wept over it" (Luke 19:41). "Who in the days of his flesh, when he had offered up prayers and supplications with strong crying and tears . . . And being made perfect, he became the author of eternal salvation" (Heb. 5:7, 9).*

Psalms 126:5, 6
5 They that sow in tears shall reap in joy.
6 He that goeth forth and weepeth, bearing precious seed, shall doubtless come again with rejoicing, bringing his sheaves with him.

- **Who is weeping over your city?**

(2) **Spiritual Warfare** (unfriendly forces)

Spiritual Warfare involves standing between Satan and man and binding the powers of Satan that have bound and blinded him from coming to the knowledge of Jesus Christ and the light of the gospel.

Eph. 6:12, 13, 18
12 For we wrestle not against flesh and blood, but against principalities, against powers, against the rulers of the darkness of this world, against spiritual wickedness in high places.
13 Wherefore take unto you the whole armour of God, that ye may be able to withstand in the evil day, and having done all, to stand.
18 Praying always with all prayer and supplication in the Spirit, and watching thereunto with all perseverance and supplication for all saints;

Acts 26:16, 18
16 I have appeared unto thee for this purpose, to make thee a minister and a witness..
18 To open their eyes, and to turn them from darkness to light, and from the power of Satan unto God, that they may receive forgiveness of sins, and inheritance among them which are sanctified by faith that is in me.

41

2 Cor. 4:3, 4
3 But even if our Gospel be hidden (obscured and covered up with a veil that hinders the knowledge of God), it is hidden [only] to those who are perishing and obscured [only] to those who are lost.
4 For the god of this world has blinded the unbelievers' minds [that they should not discern the truth], preventing them from seeing the illuminating light of the Gospel of the glory of Christ. AMP

(3) Claiming Our Personal Harvest Field

Praying for those in our circle of influence and the area of our city that is within the reach of our church:

- Against the powers of Satan that have bound and blinded the people.

- Against businesses that promote evil.

- For the deliverance and salvation of individuals that we know and also for the unnamed souls in our harvest field.

- For God to lead us to key people that will be influential in bringing many souls into the Kingdom.

Gen. 13:14, 15, 17
14 And the Lord said unto Abram, after that Lot was separated from him, Lift now thine eyes, and look from the place where thou art northward, and southward, and westward:
15 For all the land which thou seest, to thee will I give it, and to thy seed forever.
17 Arise, walk through the land in the length of it and in the breadth of it; for I will give it unto thee.

(4) Praying for God's Direction, Wisdom and Anointing

Praying for wisdom and boldness to operate in the power, dominion and authority over Satan and sickness that we have been given as a believer and a son of God.

Mark 16:17,18	*And these signs shall follow them that believe; In my name shall they **cast out devils**; they shall **lay hands on the sick,** and they **shall recover**.*
Luke 9:1	**The 12 disciples represent the fivefold ministry:** *Then he called his twelve disciples together, and gave them power and authority over all **devils**, and to cure **diseases**.*
Luke 10:1, 9, 19	**The 70 given the same power, represent the laity:** *The Lord appointed other seventy also, and sent them two and two before his face into every city . . . **Heal the sick** that are therein . . . I give you **power over all the power of the enemy** and nothing shall by any means hurt you.*

(5) Praying Promises and Prophecies into Fulfillment

This involves praying into fulfillment the promises and prophecies in God's Word regarding restoration of apostolic power, dominion and authority, and the unrestrained outpouring of God's Spirit with miracles of salvation, deliverance and healing.

The last day church, just before the coming of Jesus Christ, will not be weak and in a survival mode. But God's promise of restoration will be fulfilled and the church will be at the zenith of its glory -- exceeding that of the first century church in the book of Acts. It will be a:

- Holy, glorious, triumphant church.
- Revival church evangelizing the world with the redemption message of Jesus Christ.
- Church demonstrating the supernatural power of its Master Designer and Builder.

Like Elijah (who prayed for God's promised rain) and Daniel (who prayed for the prophecy concerning the restoration of Israel to their homeland) we must press with our prayers of intercession to birth the prophecies for restoration of apostolic ministry with intense revival and evangelism: *"The Lord working with them, and confirming the word with signs following."*

This is discussed in more detail in Section III, Chapter 2, "God Works Through Man to Perform His Will on Earth."

- **When we have taken our dominion prayer as far as we can with our human mind and understanding, we can then begin praying in the Spirit where the Spirit makes intercession for us.**

2. Praying in the Spirit and Praying with the Understanding

One of the most controversial and misunderstood concepts in God's Word (among Christians and non-Christians alike) is praying in tongues. Man's carnal evaluation and Satan's lies of intimidation, have created much resistance to this type of prayer because of the incredible power it releases into the life of a born-again believer. In the same way that many reject or avoid the Gifts of the Spirit (1 Cor. 12:1-11), because of misuses, the same approach has been taken, perhaps in greater extremes, toward praying in tongues. Praying in tongues is foolish to the natural man since the things of God cannot be understood with the carnal mind:

"But the natural man receiveth not the things of the Spirit of God: for they are foolishness unto him: neither can he know them, because they are spiritually discerned" (1 Cor. 2:14).

"But God has chosen the foolish things of the world to put to shame the wise, and God has chosen the weak things of the

45

world to put to shame the things which are mighty; and the base things of the world and the things which are despised God has chosen, and the things which are not, to bring to nothing the things that are, that no flesh should glory in His presence" (1 Cor. 1:27-29).

Just because our minds cannot understand God's ways, does not give us reason to ignore them. Tongues is a mystery to the natural man, but at the same time it is a miraculous and powerful gift. It will not only enrich our personal prayer life but will bring us into deeper intimacy and communion with the Holy Spirit.

Praying in tongues was highly prized and cherished by apostle Paul who wrote thirteen of the twenty-seven books of the New Testament. To emphasize the extreme importance of this concept, he dedicated a significant portion of 1 Corinthians 14 to its instruction. It is no coincidence that the man who spoke in tongues more than anyone, 1 Cor. 14:18, received the greatest revelation of the mysteries of Jesus Christ -- writing most of the text in the New Testament instructing us how to live the Christian life.

- **Apostle Paul's significant emphasis on the concept of praying in tongues is an invitation for us, as born-again Christians, to re-evaluate where we stand on its purpose, relevance and application in our personal devotion in prayer.**

We are living in the last of the last days just before the second coming of Jesus Christ. It is now time for the complete restoration of the apostolic ministry with power, dominion and authority over Satan and sickness, prophesied to be greater than the first century church in the book of Acts. One of the key elements that will drive and bring this to fruition will be an exponential increase in the body of Christ of praying in the Spirit.

Three Uses of Tongues in the New Testament

Before further discussion of the subject, "praying in tongues" let's first review the three different uses and purposes of tongues in the New Testament:

1. Speaking in tongues is the initial sign and evidence of receiving the gift of the Holy Ghost:

This is the second step (born of the Spirit) in the new birth experience spoken in Jesus' message to Nicodemus: *"Except a man be born of water* [baptism in Jesus name] *and of the Spirit* [baptism of the Holy Ghost]*, he cannot enter into the kingdom of God."* This new birth experience is recorded in: Acts 2:37-41 (Jews), Acts 8:14-10 (Samaritans), Acts 10:44-48 (Gentiles), and Acts 19:1-6 (John the Baptist's disciples).

2. The gift of tongues and interpretation of tongues are twin gifts that operate together:

The gift of tongues is a supernatural utterance by the Holy Spirit in a language not understood or learned by the speaker and rarely understood by the hearers. The gift of interpretation of tongues is the supernatural explanation by the Spirit of the meaning of an utterance in a known native tongue understood by the hearers. These gifts are used in a public setting to deliver a message from God for His people to understand: *"One is given the ability to speak in unknown languages, while another is given the ability to interpret what is being said. It is the one and only Spirit who distributes all these gifts"* *(1 Cor. 12:10, 11). NLT*

47

3. Praying in the Spirit is praying in tongues or unknown tongues:

Praying in the Spirit is the ability given to believers that allows them to pray in a supernatural language. It is also sometimes referred to as praying in tongues or praying in unknown tongues. Praying in the Spirit is the means by which our spirit communicates directly with God's Spirit.

Apostle Paul states in 1 Corinthians, Chapter 14, that concerning our weapons of prayer, it is vital that we pursue the use of both: (1) praying in the Spirit in an unknown tongue and (2) praying in our natural language that we can understand:

1 Cor. 14:14, 15, 18
14 For if I pray in a language I don't understand, my spirit is praying, but I don't know what I am saying.
15 Well, then, what shall I do? I will do both. I will pray in unknown tongues and also in ordinary language that everyone understands. I will sing in unknown tongues and also in ordinary language so that I can understand the praise I am giving;
18 I thank God that I "speak in tongues" privately more than any of the rest of you. TLB

15 I will pray in the spirit, and I will also pray in words I understand. I will sing in the spirit, and I will also sing in words I understand. NLT

The biblical purpose of praying in tongues is for use in the believer's own private prayer and devotion: *"I thank God that I speak in tongues more than any of you. But in a church meeting I would rather speak five understandable words to help others than ten thousand words in an unknown language"* (1 Cor. 14:18, 19).

Everyone who has received the Holy Spirit baptism can and should exercise this supernatural way of praying.

- **Praying with the understanding (known tongues) and praying in the Spirit (unknown tongues) will enrich your personal prayer life.**

Benefits of Praying in Tongues

There are numerous benefits for a believer who prays in tongues. A few are summarized below to identify some of the reasons why every believer should pray in tongues and to highlight the blessings that can be theirs through appropriating the power of praying in the Spirit.

1. Praying in tongues is the highest level of intimate communication with God.

Praying in tongues is God's method of bypassing the human mind in prayer, allowing our spirit to commune directly with His Spirit -- in a spirit-to-Spirit communication. As we pray in the Spirit, we have a high-level communication line to the Creator of the universe. Apostle Paul states: *"For he that speaketh in an unknown tongue speaketh not unto men, but unto God: for no man understandeth him; howbeit in the spirit he speaketh mysteries" (1 Cor. 14:2).*

2. Praying in tongues assist us when we are overwhelmed with burdens, problems and situations and we don't know what to say or how we should pray.

This may involve:

- Physical or spiritual needs in our life.
- Finding direction for our lives.
- Needs in the lives of family or friends.

49

- Needs of healing, deliverance or salvation for lost souls.
- Revelation and wisdom to operate as a son of God with apostolic dominion and authority over Satan and sickness, etc.

In these times, human intelligence and words fail and fall short of a solution to the need. This is when we should move to a higher level of prayer, described by apostle Paul in Romans, Chapter 8, where the Spirit takes over and prays through us and for us.

Rom. 8:26, 27
*26 The [Holy] Spirit comes to our aid and bears us up in our weakness; for we do not know what prayer to offer nor how to offer it worthily as we ought, but the Spirit goes to meet our supplication and **pleads in our behalf** with unspeakable yearnings and groanings too deep for utterance.*
*27 And He Who searches the hearts of men knows what is in the mind of the [Holy] Spirit, because the **Spirit intercedes and pleads in behalf of the saints according to and in harmony with God's will**. AMP*

*26 The Spirit helps us in our weakness. We do not know what we ought to pray for, but **the Spirit intercedes for us** with groans that words cannot express.*
*27 And he who searches our hearts knows the mind of the Spirit, because **the Spirit intercedes for the saints in accordance with God's will**. NIV*

*26 And in the same way -- by our faith -- the Holy Spirit helps us with our daily problems and in our praying. For we don't even know what we should pray for nor how to pray as we should, but the **Holy Spirit prays for us** with such feeling that it cannot be expressed in words. TLB*

3. Praying in tongues helps us discover and fulfill God's will for our lives.

Praying in the Spirit is praying in alignment with God's divine will. It is praying for the things which the Spirit desires for us to pray. Apostle Paul states in Romans 8:27, that when we pray in the Spirit, the Spirit of God intercedes for us according to the will of God. Finding and pursuing the will of God for our lives is the most important challenge and issue for a born-again Christian. Apostle Paul in 1 Corinthians 2:10, states that the Spirit searches all things, the deep things of God.

As we cooperate with God in prayer, His Spirit aligns our will with His will and gives us the direction and power to make that transition. If we are desiring something that isn't God's will for us, then His Spirit can change us and align our hearts with His purpose and plan. Praying in tongues allows us to pray in agreement with God's perfect will. We should not be afraid to embrace the will of God, because it is the only thing that will bring true joy and fulfillment in our lives.

4. Praying in tongues provides divine revelation.

Apostle Paul states in *1 Cor. 14:2: "For he that speaketh in an unknown tongue speaketh not unto men, but unto God: for no man understandeth him; howbeit **in the spirit he speaketh mysteries.**"* In the New Testament the word "mystery" does not mean mysterious as with the word in our English language. It refers to divine revelation, which is illuminated or revealed by the Spirit. Only God's Spirit can bring revelation concerning the unknown (mysteries) to us regarding His Word, His power, His will for our life and the unique circumstances we will encounter in life.

51

1 Cor. 2:10-14

10 The Spirit searcheth all things, yea, the deep things of God.

11 For what man knoweth the things of a man, save the spirit of man which is in him? even so the things of God knoweth no man, but the Spirit of God.

12 Now we have received, not the spirit of the world, but the spirit which is of God; that we might know the things that are freely given to us of God.

13 Which things also we speak, not in the words which man's wisdom teacheth, but which the Holy Ghost teacheth; comparing spiritual things with spiritual.

14 But the natural man receiveth not the things of the Spirit of God: for they are foolishness unto him: neither can he know them, because they are spiritually discerned.

5. Praying in tongues is a powerful tool that edifies and builds up our spiritual man.

"But you, beloved, build yourselves up [founded] on your most holy faith [make progress, rise like an edifice higher and higher], praying in the Holy Spirit" (Jude 20). AMP

"But you, dear friends, build yourselves up in your most holy faith and pray in the Holy Spirit" (Jude 20). NIV

Praying in the Spirit stimulates our faith. The term: "building yourself up" has the same meaning in the Greek, as that of "charging up a dead car battery." Praying in the Spirit, which results in greater faith, is God's antidote for the spirit of fear. With the absence of fear, an atmosphere is created that allows faith and the miraculous to work unrestricted in our lives and churches.

6. Praying in tongues is part of our offensive armor.

"Wherefore take unto you the whole armour of God, that ye may be able to withstand in the evil day, and having done all, to stand. Above all, taking the shield of faith, wherewith ye shall be able to quench all the fiery darts of the wicked. And take the helmet of salvation, and the sword of the Spirit, which is the word of God: **Praying always with all prayer and supplication in the Spirit***" (Eph. 6:13, 16-18).*

7. When we pray in tongues no one, including Satan, knows what we are saying.

Tongues is the language of the supernatural realm just like Spanish is the language of Mexico. *"For he that speaketh in an unknown tongue speaketh not unto men, but unto God: for no man understandeth him" (1 Cor. 14:2).* Satan knows what we are doing, but cannot understand what we are saying. Praying in tongues also gives us the advantage of privacy and confidentiality in a prayer meeting with fellow believers.

8. When we pray in tongues we minister to God, others and ourselves.

Speaking directly to God: *"For he that speaketh in an unknown tongue speaketh not unto men but unto God" (1 Cor. 14:2).*

Singing in worship to God: *"I will sing with the spirit and I will sing with the understanding" (1 Cor. 14:15).*

Ministering to others: *"Praying always with all prayer and supplication in the Spirit with all perseverance and supplication for all saints" (Eph. 6:18).*

Ministering to yourself: *"He that speaketh in an unknown tongue edifieth himself [builds himself up]" (1 Cor. 14:4).*

A Balanced and Effective Prayer Life

Praying in tongues greatly benefits our Christian walk. It is powerful, available and life-changing. It will assist us in living a victorious life. It edifies, empowers, and directs us into God's perfect will. It is a powerful tool that will not only enrich our personal prayer life but will bring us into deeper intimacy and communion with the Holy Spirit -- empowering us to minister more effectively to the needs of others.

II
Focused Prayer

"But when you pray, go into your (most) private room, and closing the door, pray to your Father, who is in secret. And when you pray, do not heap up phrases (multiply words, repeating the same ones over and over) as the Gentiles do." (Matt. 6:6, 7) AMP

1. Prayer Agendas

There is a danger of falling into a pattern of repetitious words if we do not intentionally pray focused and specific prayers. Jesus in His teaching admonishes us to be focused in our prayers and not to use vain repetitious words: *"But when ye pray, use not vain repetitions, as the heathen do: for they think that they shall be heard for their much speaking. Be not ye therefore like unto them"* (Matt. 6:7, 8).

Then in the very next verse, Jesus gave us a pattern for prayer which focused on specific things:

Matt. 6:9-13
9 After this manner therefore pray ye: Our Father which art in heaven, Hallowed be thy name.
10 Thy kingdom come. Thy will be done in earth, as it is in heaven.
11 Give us this day our daily bread.
12 And forgive us our debts, as we forgive our debtors.
13 And lead us not into temptation, but deliver us from evil: For thine is the kingdom, and the power, and the glory, forever. Amen.

The Lord's Prayer

The three positions or focuses of prayer, discussed in Chapter 1, are included in the pattern that Jesus gave His disciples.

Focus of Prayer	The Lord's Prayer	Summary Commentary
Relationship (Upward)	*Our Father which art in heaven,*	Recognizing God's sovereignty over the universe.
	Hallowed be thy name. (Holy is thy name)	Worship, honor and praise for a loving, kind, merciful, gracious, generous, faithful, awesome, supernatural, all-powerful God.
Transformation (Inward)	*Thy kingdom come.*	Recognizing God's Kingdom and asking Him to be the King of our lives.
	Thy will be done in earth, as it is in heaven.	Submitting to God's eternal will and purpose for our lives vs. our will.
Relationship (Upward)	*Give us this day our daily bread.*	Bread symbolizes everything we need to sustain life. Asking God for the things we need and recognizing that: *"Every good and perfect gift comes down from the Father above."*

The Lord's Prayer (continued)

Transformation (Inward)	*And forgive us our debts, as we forgive our debtors.*	Asking God to forgive us of our sins and to help us forgive those who have sinned against us (so that we can be forgiven).
Transformation (Inward)	*And lead us not into temptation, but deliver us from evil:*	Asking that God would help us to avoid areas that would tempt us to sin; and to give us power to resist the evil influences of the world, the flesh and the devil.
Dominion (Outward)	*For thine is the kingdom, and the power, and the glory, forever.*	Recognizing the power and glory of God's kingdom that He has imparted to us. Praying that His power, and glory would be demonstrated in our lives to reach souls in need of deliverance, healing and salvation.
Relationship (Upward)	*Amen.*	Expressing our sincere desire and confidence that our faithful God will hear and answer our prayer.

Focused Prayer

The most effective kind of prayer is focused and specific. Too often people pray in generalities. To be most effective, we need to pray focused, definite and specific prayers like a sharpshooter hitting the bull's eye of a target. If we want to be an effective prayer warrior, we need to make our prayers as specific as possible, like carefully aimed arrows. A well-aimed prayer arrow will hit the target and bring results.

The apostle James states that we do not receive an answer to our prayers because we do not ask, or we ask with the wrong motives: *"You do not have, because you do not ask. Or you do ask and yet fail to receive, because you ask with wrong purpose and motives" (James 4:2, 3). AMP*

Shut the Door

Jesus gave His disciples specific instructions on how to pray: *"But thou, when thou prayest, **enter into thy closet**, and when thou hast **shut thy door**, pray to thy Father which is in secret; and thy Father which seeth in secret shall reward thee openly" (Matt. 6:6).*

"Shutting the door" is one of the most important keys to undistracted and focused prayer. Find a quiet place, free from distractions and interruptions. But shutting the door means more than barricading ourselves in a room. When we spend time in this secret place with the God of the universe, we close the door on everything that would disturb or hinder our communication with God. We set our heart's attention on the living God. This is an act of the will, a decision to be quiet, to listen, and to be sensitive to the Spirit.

"God makes all His best people in loneliness. Do you know what the secret of praying is? Praying in secret: *When you pray, go into your inner room and shut the door."* [1]

-- From "Barnes Notes"

[**Enter into thy closet**] Every Jewish house had a place for secret devotion. Here, in secrecy and solitude, the Jew might offer his prayers, unseen by any but the Searcher of hearts. To this place, or to some similar place, our Saviour directed his disciples to retire when they wished to hold communion with Him. This is the place commonly mentioned in the New Testament as the "upper room," or the place for secret prayer.

There should be some "place" to which we may resort where no ear will hear us but "His" ear, and no eye can see us but His eye. Unless there is such a place, secret prayer will not be long or strictly maintained. It is often said that we have no such place, and can secure none. We are away from home; we are traveling; we are among strangers; we are in stages and steamboats, and how can we find such places of retirement? I answer, the desire to pray, and the love of prayer, will create such places in abundance. The Saviour had all the difficulties which we can have, but yet he lived in the practice of secret prayer. To be alone, he rose up "a great while before day," and went into a solitary place and prayed, Mark 1:35.

What excuse can they have for not praying who have a home, and who spend the precious hours of the morning in sleep, and who will practice no self-denial that they may be alone with God? O Christian! thy Saviour did it to pray for thee, too indolent and too unconcerned about thy own salvation and that of the world to practice the least self-denial in order to commune with God! How can religion live thus? How can such a soul be saved? [2]

61

Refer to the following pages for sample prayer agendas. These should be changed as needed to fit each unique situation.

The Pastor's Prayer Agenda

This is a summary of the things the pastor would like the saints to pray in their personal prayer life. It can include the things he is emphasizing in his teaching and preaching: (e.g. the mission, vision and goals of the church, faithfulness to God's house, finding God's will for working in the Kingdom, etc.).

Church Service Prayer Agenda

This is a summary of the things the pastor would like the saints to pray regarding the church services.

Parents Praying for Their Children

Chapter 2 addresses one of the most critical needs for focused prayer. And that is parents praying for their children -- their most valuable treasure.

1.1 Pastor's Prayer Agenda (for the church)

This is the pastor's request for the saints to pray each day in their private devotion for revival and evangelism in the church:

1 Pray for a renewal of revival prayer, fasting and service, that will bring restoration to the church: *"The Lord working with them, and confirming the word with signs following."*

2 Pray that we would understand the **urgency of the hour**, and that God would give us an understanding of the times in which we live. We are in the last days -- the last harvest. **Jesus is coming soon!** How much time do we have left, and what does He want us to do with that time?

3 Pray that laborers would be sent into the harvest. Jesus' only prayer request was that **we would pray for more laborers** to be sent into the harvest field.

4 Pray that our church's outreach efforts will be greatly increased:
- ✓ Revival of the love of God (love for each other and lost souls).
- ✓ Go beyond being the friendliest church to being the most loving church (friendly is easy, love is sacrifice).
- ✓ Involvement by every saint -- **"Everyone a Minister."**
- ✓ Visitors ministered to one-on-one – finding out their needs (assuring them of our prayers).
- ✓ For many souls to be delivered, saved and healed.
- ✓ Assure that new converts are accepted into our fellowship, mentored by mature saints, discipled, and established as workers in the church.

Pastor's Prayer Agenda (continued)

5 Pray for a "Revival of Obedience" in our life:
- ✓ To avoid sins of the flesh and sins of the Spirit.
- ✓ To do His perfect will:
  "Lord what wilt thou have me to do?" *(Acts 9:6)*

6 Pray **spiritual warfare** and **intercessory prayer** to destroy spiritual blindness and the strongholds of Satan that keep the lost from coming to God and being saved.

7 Pray for our pastor and church leaders.
- ✓ Pray for wisdom, knowledge, direction and anointing to lead us.
- ✓ Pray that God would raise up more spiritual leaders to assist our pastor.

8 Pray for the unity and peace of our church so that problems will not divert us from pursuing the mission of the church: "Seeking and Saving the Lost."
- ✓ In unity with the Holy Spirit
- ✓ In unity with our leaders
- ✓ In unity with one another

9 Pray for the anointing of God on all of our efforts. (Anointing is **divine ability** vs. human ability.)

10 Pray that we would always put God first in our life and our faithfulness to His house would exceed that to our employer.

11 Pray for our home and foreign missionaries.

12 Other:

1.2 Church Service Prayer Agenda

A. Focused Prayer Requests for our Church Service

	We pray that our church service would have:
1	An atmosphere of thanksgiving, praise, and worship.
2	Conviction of the sinner.
3	Anointing of the minister and saints (divine ability). Anointing of our ears to hear what the Spirit is saying to the church and to us as individuals.
4	Unity – One Mind – One Accord: ✓ In unity with the Holy Spirit. ✓ In unity with our leaders. ✓ In unity with one another.
5	God's Spirit present to provide every physical and spiritual need.
6	The Gifts of the Spirit operating in our service.
7	The Spirit of love, humility and unity flowing in the body of Christ.
8	Other:

1.2 Church Service Prayer Agenda (continued)

B. Binding and Loosing

Use the authority of Jesus name and plead His blood to bind evil spirits and release the Holy Spirit.

Bind the spirit of:	Loose the Spirit of:
✕ Fear (Doubt, Anxiety, Stress)	✓ Love, Power and a Sound Mind (2 Tim. 1:7)
✕ Disunity and Division	✓ Unity with the Holy Spirit, Our Leaders and One Another (Eph. 4:2, 3)
✕ Jealousy, Hate, Anger, Strife	✓ Love and Humility (Eph. 5:2)
✕ Heaviness (Sorrow, Depression, Hurts, Despair)	✓ Comfort and Praise (John 15:26)
✕ Error and Deception (Blindness to the Truth)	✓ Spirit of Truth (John 16:13)
✕ Anti-Christ (Anything that Exalts Itself Above Christ)	✓ Spirit of Jesus Christ (1 John 4:6)
✕ Bondage (Fears, Addictions, Sin)	✓ Liberty and Freedom (Rom. 8:15)
✕ Pride (Rebellion)	✓ Humility and Submission (Prov. 16:19)
✕ Infirmity (Oppression and Sickness)	✓ Healing and Miracles (Rom. 8:1, 2)
✕ Other:	✓ Other:

2. Our Children – Our Most Valuable Treasure

The benefits of a family altar and family devotion in a home cannot be overemphasized. There is a small window of opportunity that we have as parents, at each stage of our children's lives, to teach them and nurture them in the ways of God. And there is nothing more essential or of eternal value than investing in our children by praying for them and teaching them to pray. Helping them establish a connection with God in prayer will provide them an anchor that will stabilize and sustain them for the rest of their lives. Refer to Appendix 6, "Parenting and Prayer Personal Notes".

The Obed-edom blessing: As soon as David was established king of Israel, he made plans to return the ark of the covenant to the center of their worship in Jerusalem. In his first retrieval attempt, it was placed on an ox cart. When Uzzah reached out to steady the ark, the Lord smote him and he died. King David was afraid to bring the ark any further and he placed it in the home of Obed-edom.

67

When the ark came into Obed-edom's home, it became the tabernacle of God and his family began to receive great blessings.

2 Sam. 6:10-12
10 So David would not remove the ark of the Lord unto him into the city of David: but David carried it aside into the house of Obed-edom the Gittite.
*11 And the ark of the Lord continued in the house of Obed-edom the Gittite three months: and **the Lord blessed Obed-edom, and all his household.***
*12 And it was told king David, saying, **The Lord hath blessed the house of Obed-edom, and all that pertaineth unto him, because of the ark of God.** So David went and brought up the ark of God from the house of Obed-edom into the city of David with gladness.*

-- From "Adam Clarke's Commentary"

The Targum [Aramaic version of the Bible] ends this chapter thus: *"And the Word of the Lord blessed Obed-edom, and his children, and his grand-children; and his wife conceived, and his eight daughters-in-law and He blessed and increased greatly all that belonged to him."*[1]

The New Covenant in the New Testament makes us the temple of God with His Spirit dwelling in us: *"Ye are the temple of God, and the Spirit of God dwelleth in you."* When we dedicate our homes (like Obed-edom) to God with devotion of prayer and the Word, special blessings from God come to our homes and our families.

2.1 Praying for Our Children

There is great value in parents binding together around the most valuable possession they have in common. And that is their children – their greatest treasure. The most important and challenging responsibility of a parent is to nurture, train and lead their children in the ways of righteousness: *"Bring them up in the nurture and admonition of the Lord" (Eph. 6:4).* There is nothing more important in this world than the assurance of our children's salvation. Since prayer is the best thing we can do for our children, it would be very beneficial to join a prayer team that prays focused prayers for the spiritual and physical needs of our children.

Prayer Teams: Special purpose prayer teams are groups of people that rally around a common need or challenge in their lives. These teams do not need to meet regularly as a group, but are connected through a common burden. They may meet together as a group once or twice a year, but will come together and stay connected on an ongoing basis through the telephone and social media (E-mail, text, Facebook). Some of these may be temporary teams to address one-time needs while others may be permanent to address ongoing challenges and needs.

Jesus Christ declares that He will meet with His children when they come together in unity and harmony. Unified agreement in the body of Christ brings His very presence into our midst with answers to our prayers and fulfillment of our needs.

Matt. 18:19, 20
*19 Again I tell you, if **two of you on earth agree (harmonize together)** about whatever [anything and everything] they may*

ask, it will come to pass and be done for them by My Father in heaven.
*20 For wherever **two or three are gathered** (drawn together as My followers) in My name, there I am in the midst of them. AMP*

Opportunities abound to advance the power of prayer by creating and engaging special purpose prayer teams. One of the most important is parents praying for their children. This is an important prayer and support team for the parents of children in the three different stages of life:

- The critical decade (ages 16-26).

- Adolescence (ages 11-15).

- Young children in their formative years (ages 1-10).

Each of these age groups present different opportunities and challenges to nurture, train and support our most precious gift -- our children.

Prov. 22:6
Train up a child in the way he should go; and when he is old, he will not depart from it.

- **Teach a child to pray when he is young, and when he is old he will still be talking to God in prayer.**

- **Kids today don't have a prayer -- without parents who pray.**

Parent's Statement and Pledge to Our Children

You are the most important treasure in our lives. Nothing, other than Jesus Christ, comes close. Working for God and helping others will mean nothing if one of you are lost. We declare war on Satan and every evil forces in the world. We will fight on our knees for your eternal salvation. We pledge to fast and pray for the critical issues and decisions you will be facing as you grow from a child to an adult.

We will continue to carry a burden and do everything possible to influence you for the best as you begin to make your own life decisions. If we should suddenly pass from this life without the chance to say good-bye, there is one message we leave you. And that is: **"Be there!"** Make that the number one goal in your life to be there. Be there, because we will be looking for you on that resurrection morning. Don't let anything deter you from keeping that appointment. We will be waiting for you just inside the Eastern Gate. Seeing you there is the number one priority in our life.

I have prayed this prayer regarding my children and undoubtedly other parents have prayed the same: "We love you so much that we sincerely pray, if mistakes you make in life are due to our failure to teach you or to be the right example, we ask that any resulting punishment would be placed on us and not you. We also pray like Thomas Paine, one of the founding fathers of our nation: "If there must be trouble, let it be in my day, that my child may have peace."

Refer to the following pages for sample prayer agendas regarding parents praying for their children and praying for one another.

The following Sub-chapter, 2.2 "Teaching Our Children to Pray", provides a brief summary of some things to consider in teaching and assisting children in the following age groups to pray:

- Children in the critical decade (ages 16-26).

- Children in the adolescent years (ages 11-15).

- Children in the formative years (ages 1-10).

Parents and Sunday school teachers alike must continuously modify their teaching methods and content regarding prayer as the children under their care grow and mature in their understanding.

Parents Prayer Agenda for Children in the Critical Decade (ages 16 – 26)

We pray that our children will:

1 Develop a godly character and pursue God's will for their lives.

2 Remember and honor the heritage of truth and faith handed down to them by previous generations and then be diligent in teaching it to their children. Come to realize early in life that Jesus Christ is the only source and true meaning of life.

3 Learn to trust God and depend on Him in times of difficulty and trial.

4 Choose the right lifelong companion that will partner with them in pursuing God's will for their lives.

5 Choose the right career, and find a job that will allow them to make a good living but not interfere with being faithful to God's house and work.

6 We will plead the name and blood of Jesus every day for their protection from: (1) evils and temptations of this world, (2) sickness and disease, (3) harm and danger.

7 We will pray that whatever they do, they will put God first in their lives and do His will.

8 Other specific needs for each individual child.

Note: The Parents Prayer Agenda above for children in the critical decade (ages 16-26) should be changed as appropriate to fit the specific needs of children in their adolescent years (ages 11-15) and those in their formative years (ages 1-10).

Parents Praying for One Another

In addition to praying for our children, another focus of this prayer group will be parents praying for one another.

	Parents will pray for one another that we will:
1	Have godly wisdom to help lead and guide our children in the fear and admonition of God through this critical era of their lives.
2	Know how much to hold on and how much to let go, as our children move out of the arena of adolescence and into the world of adult responsibilities.
3	React to our children's problems through earnest prayer. But more important be proactive and pray for future decisions and issues before they become problems and pitfalls.
4	Successfully pass on the torch of truth to our children.
5	Be a support group to one another and bear one another's burden for our children.
6	Other.

2.2 Teaching Our Children to Pray

Teaching our children to pray is one of our most important roles as a parent. One of the first ways our children learn the importance of prayer is hearing us pray. Our children need to know early in their lives that they can talk to God just like they talk to their parents or a best friend. They need to understand that God is attentive to what they have to say; and that He is always there to listen, whether they are at school, in the car, or at church.

One of the benefits of praying with your child is getting a glimpse into what your child is thinking or is worried about. As you ask them about their concerns and prayer requests, you will get a glimpse into their soul. This will allow you to identify areas where you can focus your prayers and parenting skills.

- **Prayer is the greatest tool you can give your child to ensure they will enjoy a successful natural and spiritual life.**

-- From "Children's Ministry Magazine"

Prayer habits that last a lifetime are most often formed in early childhood. That's why it's so critical to teach young children how to pray. As with most spiritual disciplines, prayer is caught more than it's taught. As parents model meaningful prayer lives, kids will learn how they, too, can talk to their Creator.[2]

- **The earlier the parent starts in the process of training and mentoring their child in the essentials of prayer the more successful the outcome.**

-- From "Prayer Activities for Children"

Starting and ending each day with prayer is a great way to get children tuned into their special relationship with God without distractions. To use this method as a group activity in Sunday School, do the "before" prayer at the start of class, and the "after" prayer close to the time class ends. At home, praying before leaving for school, day care, or to spend the day with a babysitter, can help children of all ages start the day off right. This is a great time to pray for teachers, friends, and for help with classes or peer relationships. If your child is stressed or anxious about the day ahead, pray with them to give their cares up to God and to release their concerns so that they trust God for what the day will bring.[3]

2.2.1 Children in the Critical Decade (ages 16-26)

Some of the most dramatic and life-impacting decisions will occur during the years of youth between 16 and 26. During this period, a person is transformed from a youth (still living at home depending on their parents for help and guidance in spiritual, natural and financial issues) to a full-grown adult earning a living and taking full charge of their own life. Most of the decisions that are made in this critical decade will shape the rest of their life. Some of these life-shaping decisions include:

- What am I to do with my life?

- Will I pursue higher education (what and where)?

- Who will I marry that will be my lifelong companion and pursue the will of God for our lives?

- What occupation and career should I select and pursue?

- What values and principles will be established to govern my life?

- Will I hold to the doctrines and holiness concepts passed to me from my parents, pastors and teachers.

All of these decisions and choices are extremely difficult. Mistakes and errors made during this critical decade can undermine all that will follow. There will be pressures and temptations in college and the workplace that previous generations did not face.

Prophetic events indicate that our children may be the last generation before the second coming of Jesus Christ. We must ensure that there is nothing lost in passing the torch of truth to those who will anchor the last lap of the Christian race. We must do everything possible to example and teach our children the importance of prayer -- assuring that the church of tomorrow is left in dedicated godly hands.

Teaching Prayer Concepts for Ages 16-26

This age group can grasp prayer concepts at the adult level. The principles laid out in Chapter 1, "Chart P-3: Relationship Prayer", "Chart P-4: Transformation Prayer" and "Chart P-5: Dominion Prayer" can be used to teach and assist this age group in developing their own personal prayer agenda and balanced prayer life.

2.2.2 Children in the Adolescent Years (ages 11-15)

Adolescence is a period of transition when the individual changes physically and psychologically from a child to an adult. During no other period does the individual undergo such a sudden and drastic change in such a short time; and at no other age are they less prepared to cope with the problems that this change brings.

It is a period when rapid physiological and psychological changes demand for new social roles to take place. The adolescents, due to these changes, often face a number of crises and dilemmas in dealing with the demands of significant adjustment to these physical and social changes.

Adolescence involves a significant amount of stress and strain from peer pressure. It brings many ambiguities in life. During this phase, one really does not know where he or she stands. It is believed that this uncertainty about one's role causes many conflicts. It is a well-known fact that delinquency rates soar during the period of adolescence; that suicides become increasingly prevalent; and that drug and alcohol addictions have their beginning.

The Potential of an Adolescent: Historians say that David was just a young boy between the ages of 11 and 16 when he was anointed king; killed a lion and bear single-handedly; and killed the giant Goliath, with a stone and a sling (with God's anointing). The Bible confirms this young age: *"Don't be ridiculous!" Saul replied. "There's no way you can fight this Philistine and possibly win! You're only a boy, and he's been a man of war since his youth" (1 Sam. 17:33). NLT*

The prophet Samuel was brought to the temple, as a young child, by his mother and left there to serve the priest. God

79

spoke to him at an early age regarding His judgment on the existing priesthood of Eli and his sons. According to the historian Josephus, Samuel was ten years old when he came to the temple and twelve years old when God spoke to him.

Teaching Prayer Concepts for Ages 11-15

The principles laid out in Chapter 1, "Three Basic Parts of Prayer" (Charts P-3, P-4, P-5) can be modified by parents and teachers and used to assist the adolescent child in developing their own personal prayer agenda and balanced prayer life:

- Relationship prayer (acknowledging God's greatness, thanking Him for blessings, asking Him to supply our needs and help us solve our problems).

- Transformation prayer (asking God for forgiveness and to be changed to be like Him).

- Dominion prayer (praying for the needs of others).

Also, a visual like Chart C-1, "Teaching Young Children the A, B, C's of Prayer", at the end of this chapter, may be used at the individual or classroom level to assist in helping the younger children in this group to understand the three basic parts of prayer and teaching them to pray.

2.2.3 Children in the Formative Years (ages 1-10)

Shocking evidence points to how the foundations of social, emotional, intellectual and moral values are wired extremely early into a child's brain. In the first ten years of life, basic moral and spiritual values have already been set almost as immovable as concrete in the little child's mind. What parents and teachers of young children do with a young child affects their entire life far more than most vaguely realize. The spiritual potential of a young child is significant and is often overlooked by parents and teachers alike.

Children learn quickly and the normal child learns very easily! One word, positive or negative, can plant an idea into a tender, young mind that will never be erased! This is why Christian parents and Christian teachers of small children must diligently seek the face of God for the precious souls entrusted by the Lord to their care. **There is a subtle, limited window of time** when we have the grand opportunity to plant seeds of righteousness and godliness into the hearts of small children.

An amazing study in Medical Science research has found a newborn infant's brain contains a language room. The little window of entrance to the infant's language room is wide open at birth. The newborn is universal. He may learn Russian, Spanish, English, Japanese, or any other language fluently, even at an incredibly young age! His learned language will inevitably depend upon what he hears and is taught by example! He learns what he is exposed to. **Will your child learn the language of prayer and the Word of God?**

The language room window in the baby's brain, this study revealed, is almost completely closed by the time the child reached puberty or adolescence, age twelve to fourteen. After this age, it has been proven, it becomes much more difficult

81

for the human being to learn a language. Before a child reaches adolescence they are totally open to God and it is much easier to teach a child to verbalize their own prayer. After that the factors of self-consciousness and self-will become barriers to overcome.

Teaching Prayer Concepts for Ages 1-10

The principles laid out in Chapter 1, "Three Basic Parts of Prayer" can be used by parents and teachers to assist a child in developing their own personal prayer agenda and balanced prayer life. The parent or teacher will need to bring this content down to the child's level to match their age and level of understanding. This will need to be changed to fit the child as he grows and matures.

To bring prayer down to the small child's level we must understand that for the most part, their prayer must be expressed with few words, in short and essential phrases. For example:

Relationship prayer:
"Thank you Jesus for giving us food."
"Thank you Jesus for my mom and dad."
"Jesus, please protect and keep us safe."

Transformation prayer:
"Jesus, please forgive me for being mean to my brother."
"Jesus, please help me to be good."
"Dear Jesus, please help me to be more like you."

Dominion prayer:
"Jesus, please save my friend Joey."
"Jesus, please heal my dad."
"Jesus, please protect and bless the missionaries."

Before the child can talk, they are listening and absorbing everything they hear. During this time the parent should verbalize these simple prayers while holding them or kneeling with them. When they can talk, they should help them verbalize their prayers in their own words. Getting them used to praying out loud is much easier at this tender innocent age before they experience the self-consciousness and awkward feelings of being unsure about themselves that comes with adolescents.

Prayer Objects: One way to dispel the thoughts of "nothing to pray for" or "prayer is boring", is to use objects that make prayer more visible and active for all age groups. Using a visible object, such as a world globe, will reinforce that God is everywhere and He can answer a prayer we pray for others half way around the world – especially when we pray for missionaries. Using a prayer wall to record prayer requests and answers to prayer will reinforce the importance and power of prayer. A walk or drive through a neighborhood will help your children identify those in need of our prayers.

A chart, like the one on the following page, may be used at the individual or classroom level to assist in helping young children understand:
- That God is big and powerful and He can do anything.
- That God is so close that they can touch Him in prayer.
- The three basic parts of prayer.

To personalize this chart, color sticky notes can be added at the bottom of this chart under the relevant category to identify the child's unique prayer request. Also, the parent may want to take pictures of their children and place over the photos provided.

Chart C-1
Teaching Children the A, B, C's of Prayer

I am so big and strong that I can do anything!

I am so close that you can touch me in prayer!

- Thanking and praising Jesus for His blessings.
- Asking Jesus for the things I need.

- Asking Jesus to forgive me.
- Asking Jesus to help me be more like Him.

- Praying for others in need.
- Praying for children in other countries.

Thank You

Change Me

Help Others

3. Driving Force for Fervent and Effective Prayer

Prayer is the key to our relationship with God and our power as a New Testament Christian, but burdens are the primary force that drives us to our knees in earnest, fervent prayer:

- Our burdens.
  - Burden for others.
    - Burden of the Lord.

Abraham Lincoln stated regarding his burdens in life: "I have been driven to my knees many times by the overwhelming conviction that I had nowhere else to go."

Without a burden, nothing significant will be accomplished in the Kingdom of God. One of the fundamental requirements for miracles is that our actions of prayer and care for those in need must be driven by a burden.

Refer to PowerPoint Chart B-1, **"Burden + Prayer + Care = Miracles"**, on the following page.

Chart B-1

3.1 Our Burdens

Burdens created by trouble and trials are tools that God often uses to change us and strengthen our faith and trust in Him. At other times, these are sent by God to correct, humble, and send us to our knees in prayer.

Psalms 25:17, 18
17 The troubles of my heart are enlarged: O bring thou me out of my distresses.
18 Look upon mine affliction and my pain; and forgive all my sins.

Psalms 119:136, 153
136 Rivers of waters run down mine eyes, because they keep not thy law.
153 Consider mine affliction, and deliver me: for I do not forget thy law.

Isa. 43:1, 2
1 But now thus saith the Lord that created thee ... Fear not: for I have redeemed thee, I have called thee by thy name; thou art mine.
2 When thou passest through the waters, I will be with thee; and through the rivers, they shall not overflow thee: when thou walkest through the fire, thou shalt not be burned; neither shall the flame kindle upon thee.

Prayer and burdens are partners with trial. Trials often drive us to a deeper prayer life. Troubles help us recognize our frailty and our need of God. When going through trials, prayer will deliver us or provides strength to endure.

Trouble is common to man. Job said, *"Man that is born of a woman is of few days, and full of trouble."* Apostle Paul stated, *"It is through many hardships and tribulations that we would enter the Kingdom of God."* Apostle Peter exclaimed, *"Beloved, think it not strange concerning the fiery trial which is to try you, as though some strange thing happened unto you: But rejoice, inasmuch as ye are partakers of Christ's sufferings."*

Without exception to age or station in life; there are unlimited varieties of problems, troubles and trials. No two people have the same trouble under the same circumstances. God does not deal with any two of His children exactly the same, just as we parents do not approach our children exactly the same.

Trouble is under control of our heavenly Father and it is a common way for God to fulfill His purpose in perfecting His saints. Trial and testing prove us, and makes us stronger. It makes us better when we submit to the pressure of the Potter's hand on our lives.

In the beginning the angels were created beings, never experiencing trial, and one-third of them sinned and fell from heaven. Now God's plan includes trial and testing for every child of God before they inherit the glories of heaven.

Rev. 7:13, 14
13 What are these which are arrayed in white robes?
*14 And I said unto him, sir, thou knowest. And he said to me, these are they which came out of **great tribulation,** and have washed their robes, and made them white in the blood of the Lamb.*

God sometimes lets trials come into our lives because we have placed our trust in other things -- careers, possessions, success in life, etc. God gets our attention as problems come for which we have no answer. When this happens, we feel a more pressing need to pray. During these times, we can find shelter in the Rock of Ages -- a place of prayer to strengthen and sustain us until the storm is over.

More is to be learned in turbulence than in peaceful times. King David said, *"In the valley he restoreth my soul."* We should thank God for trials that have brought correction, drawn us closer to Him and made us more sensitive to His Spirit.

No great victory is possible without a great battle, or a miracle without a problem. It is not God's will for us to just survive; that would mean defeat. But God's higher purpose for trials is to develop our Christian character.

As Christians, we often refer to this process as a burden. God works through our burdens to empty us of ourselves and fill us with more of Him. For this to happen, we must embrace the cross, allowing it to fulfill His intended purpose of changing our lives. It is a great comfort to know our heavenly Father has invited us to place our cares on Him. In the most difficult of times, when we have no strength, He will carry us.

Psalms 55:22
Cast your burden on the Lord *[releasing the weight of it] and He will sustain you; He will never allow the [consistently] righteous to be moved (made to slip, fall, or fail). AMP*

1 Peter 5:7
Casting the whole of your care *[all your anxieties, all your worries, all your concerns, once and for all]* **on Him,** *for He cares for you affectionately and cares about you watchfully. AMP*

Our heavenly Father desires for us to get beyond our own

burdens and focus on the **burdens of others.** As we start praying for and ministering to the burdens of others, God will work on the resolution to our own burdens and problems.

For more on the discussion of why we experience burdens and suffering, refer to Section III, Chapter 3: When the Answer to Prayer is "No" or "Wait."

3.2 Burden for Others

To please our heavenly Father, we must follow His selfless example of caring for others and bearing their burdens.

1 John 3:17, 18
17 But whoso hath this world's good, and seeth his brother have need, and shutteth up his bowels of compassion from him, how dwelleth the love of God in him?
18 My little children, let us not love in word, neither in tongue; but **in deed** *and in truth.*

When we have the true love and compassion of Christ in our life, our burden for others in need will be manifest by praying for and ministering to those needs.

The Church as a Flock of Sheep

The Bible compares the church to a flock of sheep. Our over shepherd (our pastor) will answer to God for those under his care. We must honor those whom He has placed over us for they watch for our souls and will be held accountable. Therefore, we should pray for and thank God for our leaders.

Acts 20:28
And now beware! Be sure that you feed and **shepherd God's flock** *-- his church, purchased with his blood -- for the Holy Spirit is holding you responsible as overseers. TLB*

Jesus Christ refers to Himself as the good Shepherd who died for us; purchasing our pardon and salvation with His own blood.

John 10:11, 14
11 I am the good shepherd: the good shepherd giveth his life for the sheep.
14 I am the good shepherd, and know my sheep, and am known of mine.

Often overlooked is the importance of the relationship of the sheep in the flock. We are commanded to bear each other's burdens: *"Bear ye one another's burdens, and so fulfill the law of Christ" (Gal. 6:2).*

Two kinds of people comprise the church -- those suffering in trial and those experiencing victory. Those living in victory should minister to the hurting: *"We then that are strong ought to bear the infirmities of the weak, and not to please ourselves" (Rom. 15:1).*

The cycles of life deal all of us similar hurts. Everyone, at some time, will need compassion and care. We must find those crying beneath our steeple, inside the church, and minister to them. The pastor cannot accomplish this alone -- everyone must be involved.

A sobering thought, indeed, is to know without our participation some people will never be touched. **When the in-reach of the church is effective, the outreach of the church will be more effective.** We must become a family of New Testament Christians who pray for each other and carry each other's burdens.

Halfway through a race involving handicapped children, one

boy fell down and cried out. Those ahead, turned around, went back and picked him up. With their arms locked around each other, they all made it across the finish line together. It did not matter who finished first; what was important was that they all finished the race.

As Christians, when someone falls or is wounded, we need to restore them. It has been said that Christians are the only colony who kill their wounded. This is not intentional; it is just that the burdens and busyness of our lives cause neglect and unconcern. When this happens, we are not functioning as the body of Christ.

We get in our individual car, drive down our individual street, to our individual church, sit in our individual pew, nod our individual head to our individual sermon, take our individual blessing, get back in our individual car, and return to our individual home.

That is not New Testament Christianity. Christianity is where God's children are called into community just like a family. The early church went from house to house and had all things in common. They were the family of God; bearing one another's burdens. Apostle Paul exhorts in his letter to the Romans: *"Rejoice with them that do rejoice, and weep with them that weep"*. Some people claim they don't need to attend every church service. But God saved us for an unselfish calling to encourage, pray for and minister to the hurting: *"He hath saved us, and called us with an holy calling"*:

  - If our unsaved parent or sibling was going to attend church for the first time, we would inconvenience ourselves in any way to be there.

- If our unsaved friend was going to be at church, we would be there.

- **Someone's parent, sibling, or friend in need will possibly be in every church service; and if the pure agape love of God is flowing in our lives, we will treat them the same as our kin or friend.**

Blessings from God are great; but we receive a much greater one when God flows through us to someone in need. If we get a revelation of this concept, our faithfulness to God's house will be without compromise.

As we minister to the needs of others, our burden will escalate to the next level -- the **burden of the Lord.**

3.3 Burden of the Lord

God gave His Word to describe His great love for man. It is a gigantic Love Letter recorded over several thousand years by thirty-nine writers. But to reinforce His message, He came to earth and displayed **His burden** as a Son of man walking in human shoes.

The burden of the Lord was prophesied by Old Testament prophets and then exampled for us in a real life drama as Jesus Christ carried out His earthly ministry.

Isa. 53:3, 4, 11, 12
3 He is despised and rejected of men; ***a man of sorrows,
and acquainted with grief.***
4 Surely ***he hath borne our griefs, and carried our
sorrows.***
11 He shall see of the ***travail of his soul,*** *and shall be
satisfied:*

*12 ... He hath **poured out his soul unto death:** and he was numbered with the transgressors; and he bare the sin of many, and made **intercession for the transgressors.***

Matt. 8:16, 17
16 When the even was come, they brought unto him many that were possessed with devils: and he cast out the spirits with his word, and healed all that were sick:
*17 That it might be fulfilled which was spoken by Esaias the prophet, saying, **Himself took our infirmities, and bare our sicknesses.***

Mark 14:34
*And saith unto them, My soul is **exceeding sorrowful unto death:** tarry ye here, and watch.*

Luke 19:41
*And when he was come near, he beheld the city, and **wept over it.***

Heb. 5:7
*Who in the days of his flesh, when he had offered up **prayers and supplications with strong crying and tears.***

The shortest, but very powerful verse in the Bible: *"Jesus wept"*, was recorded by the apostle John when Jesus saw Mary and Martha weeping at their brother's tomb.

- **The Lord carried our burden and now He asks that we carry His burden for His lost world.**

The burden of the Lord concerns what Jesus would be doing if He were still here on the earth. His mission is not complete and it is His burden that we would carry on His mission and ministry in reaching a lost world.

- **Prophecies in the Old Testament were sometimes called "The burden of the Lord", for God burdened the prophet with His Word and with its execution.**

-- From "The Pulpit Commentary"

When God gave the prophet a message to declare concerning some place, some person, some nation, it was a burden to the prophet. He felt its solemn weight and responsibility. And he who shall be a rejoicing reaper in the Lord's harvest field is one to whom his sacred toil has been the **burden of the Lord** to him.

This burden is made up of a deep sense of:
- His own insufficiency for the work.
- The urgent need for the work to be done.
- The shortness of time which remains for this work to be done.
- The heavy responsibility resting upon him to be faithful in the work (2 Cor. 5:11).

There may or may not be tears upon his face, but there certainly will be in his heart. Often will he weep there. These are the men who do the Lord's work, and win souls for Him.[1]

- **The burden of the Lord involves bringing to pass His promises and prophecies. If this is not happening, it may be that we have not met the requirements for their fulfillment through intercessory prayer.**

Spiritual gridlock sometimes occurs when we are waiting for God to fulfill His promises; and He is waiting on us to birth them through intercessory prayer.

The Burden of the Lord for the Restoration of His Church

Prophecy concerning the restoration of the church illustrates what the church should be like in the endtime. The calendar indicates we are in the final milestone of the 2,000 year Church Age -- the midnight hour preceding the coming of Jesus Christ.

The complete restoration of the apostolic ministry with signs, wonders and miracles will occur when we pray into fruition the burden of the Lord like Elijah and Daniel. This is discussed in more detail in Chapter 1, Section III.

- Elijah prayed a burdened travailing prayer to end the devastating three-year drought in Israel because of their sin. God answered with a deluge of refreshing rain to restore the parched land of Israel.

- Daniel took action, understanding it was God's prophesied time for restoration of Israel from Babylonian captivity to their homeland. He gave birth to the burden of the Lord through fasting and intercessory prayer.

Many times when a prophecy has not been fulfilled, it is because it is not yet God's time. But today we are living at the end of time (the last of the last days) and it is time for the complete restoration of the church. If we are to experience the restoration of apostolic ministry, we must become burdened with the burden of the Lord manifested through our sacrifice of prayer, fasting and service.

Who will carry the burden of the Lord? Who will weep over their city like Jesus? Who will pray intercessory prayers for a great revival that can transcend the book of Acts? The world deserves to see a pure and holy local church fulfilling the burden of the Lord. The burden of the first century church transmitted a fire and energy unequaled in almost 20 centuries. Just reading the book of Acts, we feel the intensity, and zeal of its revival and evangelism.

Now is time for great worldwide revival, including North America. It is happening in some foreign lands where the deceitfulness of riches and prosperity doesn't distract people from putting God first and loving Him completely. The church and their great God are all they have. He is their only hope in time and eternity and we must embrace that same truth.

This will happen in our churches when the **burden of the Lord** drives us to our knees. Then we will stop struggling with what and how to pray. The Spirit will be helping us pray -- praying into fruition the promises and prophecies of God's Word.

-- From "The Pulpit Commentary"

A Christian church may be formed after the apostolic model, and its constitution may be irreproachably scriptural, but it may fall into spiritual apathy, and care for nothing but its own edification. A single human soul, with an ear sensitive to "the still sad music of humanity," with a heart to feel the weight of "**the burden of the Lord,**" with courage to attempt great things for Christ and for men, with the faith that "removes mountains," may be of far more value to the world than such an apathetic and inactive church.[1]

The burden of the Lord encompasses His work around the world. We should have a worldwide burden, but we must first carry a burden at the local level, where we can be personally involved and make an immediate difference.

The vital importance of prayer was emphasized by God when He referred to His house as a house of prayer:

Speaking through the prophet Isaiah He says: "Even them will I bring to my holy mountain, and make them joyful in my house of prayer: their burnt offerings and their sacrifices shall be accepted upon mine altar; for mine house shall be called an house of prayer for all people." (Isa. 56:7)

Speaking through the Gospel writers, Matthew, Mark and Luke, He tell us: "Is it not written, My house shall be called of all nations the house of prayer; but ye have made it a den of thieves." (Matt 21:13, Mark 11:17, Luke 19:46)

III
The Vital Importance of Prayer

"Behold, I stand at the door, and knock: if any man hear my voice, and open the door, I will come in to him, and will sup with him, and he with me."
(Rev. 3:20)

* * * * *

"My sheep hear my voice, and I know them, and they follow me." (John 10:27)

* * * * *

The success of our walk with God is dependent on consistently completing the communication cycle: talking to God in prayer and listening to His voice through the Word and other ways that He speaks.

1. Prayer Tunes Our Spiritual Ear to Hear and Understand God's Voice

In any electronic communication device there is a transmitter and a receiver. No matter how strong the transmitter, the receiver must be turned on and tuned in to receive the message.

The transmitter of God's voice is strong and powerful: *"The voice of the Lord thundereth . . . the voice of the Lord is powerful . . . the voice of the Lord breaketh the cedars of Lebanon" (Psalms. 29:3-5).* *"My word is like a fire? saith the Lord; and like a hammer that breaketh the rock in pieces" (Jer. 23:9).* *"The Word of God is **powerful** and sharper than any two-edged sword" (Heb. 4:12).* But it takes prayer to tune our spiritual receiver to receive and understand God's message. It takes prayer to open our spiritual ears to hear with clarity what God is speaking to us.

Seven time in the Gospels, after Jesus had finished teaching, He admonished His audience: *"He that hath ears to hear, let him hear."* Eight times in the book of Revelation it is recorded: *"He that hath an ear, let him hear what the Spirit saith unto the churches.*" We know this is not speaking of our natural ears but our spiritual ears.

Jer. 5:21
Hear now this, O foolish people, and without understanding; which have eyes, and see not; which have ears, and hear not: AMP

Matt. 13:13, 14
13 This is the reason that I speak to them in parables: because having the power of seeing, they do not see; and having the power of hearing, they do not hear, nor do they grasp and understand.
14 In them indeed is the process of fulfillment of the prophecy of Isaiah, which says: You shall indeed hear and hear but never grasp and understand; and you shall indeed look and look but never see and perceive. AMP

1 Cor. 2:14
The natural man receiveth not the things of the Spirit of God: for they are foolishness unto him: neither can he know them, because they are they are spiritually discerned

- **The Word of God alone produces information. This is the reason there are hundreds of religions that claim the Bible as the basis for their beliefs. But God's Word illuminated by the Spirit, through prayer, will produce understanding and revelation. Revelation will affirm truth and create transformation in the life of a believer.**

- **The success of our walk with God is dependent on consistently completing the communication cycle: talking to God in prayer and listening to His voice through the Word and other ways that He speaks.**

Preparing Our Hearts to Hear and Receive God's Word

Jesus in the parable of the sower describes four types of ground where the Word of the seed is sown:

(1) Wayside: hears the Word but the seed is stolen by the enemy before it takes root in the heart.

(2) Stony ground: hears and receives the Word with joy, but because there is no depth of root becomes offended when there is tribulation or persecution.

(3) Thorny ground: hears and receives the Word, but the cares of this world, and the deceitfulness of riches, choke the Word, and they become unfruitful.

(4) Good ground: hears, receives and understands the Word. With understanding and revelation of the Word, they begin to bear fruit and reap a harvest -- some a hundredfold, some sixty, some thirty.

This parable of Jesus is often used as it applies to a sinner's response to the Word of God. While this is true, it also applies as much or more so to us as Christians; because our lives must constantly be cleansed and transformed by the Word.

John 17:17
Make them pure and holy through teaching them your words of truth. TLB

1 Tim. 4:16
Take heed unto thyself, and unto the doctrine; continue in them: for in doing this thou shalt both save thyself, and them that hear thee.

2 Tim. 3:14, 17
But continue thou in the things which thou hast learned and hast been assured of . . . That the man of God may be perfect, throughly furnished unto all good works.

The prophets Hosea and Jeremiah speak of preparing the heart to receive the Word of God by breaking up the hard, unplowed ground of the heart through repentance and seeking God in prayer.

Hosea 10:12
Sow to yourselves in righteousness, reap in mercy; break up your fallow ground: for it is time to seek the Lord, till he come and rain righteousness upon you.

Jer. 4:3, 4
3 For thus saith the Lord to the men of Judah and Jerusalem, Break up your fallow ground, and sow not among thorns.
4 Circumcise yourselves to the Lord, and take away the foreskins of your heart, ye men of Judah and inhabitants of Jerusalem.

3 The Lord is saying to the men of Judah and Jerusalem, Plow up the hardness of your hearts; otherwise the good seed will be wasted among the thorns.
4 Cleanse your minds and hearts, not just your bodies. TLB

-- From "Adam Clarke's Commentary"

[*Break up your fallow ground*] Fallow ground is either that which, having been once tilled, has lain long uncultivated; or, ground slightly ploughed. Ye have been long uncultivated in righteousness; let true repentance break up your fruitless and hardened hearts; and when the seed of the Word of life is sown in them, take heed that worldly cares and concerns do not arise, and, like thorns, choke the good seed.

[*Circumcise yourselves*] Put away everything that has a tendency to grieve the Spirit of God, or to render your present holy resolutions unfruitful.[1]

-- From "Matthew Henry's Commentary"

[*Break up your fallow-ground.*] They must do by their hearts as they do by their ground that they expect any good of; they must plough it up. An unconvinced unhumbled heart is like fallow-ground, ground untilled, unoccupied. It is ground capable of improvement; but it is fallow; it is unfruitful, is overgrown with thorns and weeds, which are the natural product of the corrupt heart; and, if it be not renewed with grace, rain and sunshine are lost upon it, Heb. 6:7,8. We must search our hearts, let the Word of God divide (as the plough does) between the joints and the marrow, Heb. 4:12. We must rend our hearts, Joel 2:13. We must pluck up by the roots those corruptions which, as thorns, choke both our endeavors and our expectations, Hos. 10:12.

[*Circumcise yourselves to the Lord, and take away the foreskins of your heart.*] They must do that to their souls which was done to their bodies when they were taken into covenant with God. Mortify the flesh and the lusts of it. Pare off that superfluity of naughtiness which hinders your receiving with meekness the engrafted Word, James 1:21. Devote and consecrate yourselves unto the Lord, to be to him a peculiar people.[2]

This process of preparing our hearts to hear, understand and obey God's voice must be repeated in a continuous cycle in our lives if we are to mature and be productive in the Kingdom. Apostle Paul says it is an endless process: *"I die daily" (1 Cor. 15:31). "Let us lay aside every weight, and the sin which doth so easily beset us, and let us run with patience the race that is set before us. Looking unto Jesus the author and finisher of our faith" (Heb. 12:1, 2).*

Hearing the Voice of God

Jesus gives us these assuring words in the Gospel of John: *"My sheep hear my voice, and I know them, and they follow me: And I give unto them eternal life; and they shall never perish, neither shall any man pluck them out of my hand."*

"My sheep" indicates that God's voice is for everyone and not just ministers. Everyone can have a relationship with God where they can talk to Him and they can hear His voice.

In the very first book in the Bible, at the dawn of creation, we see God's desire and plan to communicate with man: *"And they heard the voice of the Lord God walking in the garden in the cool of the day"* (Gen. 1:8).

In the very last book in the Bible we see God's desire and effort to communicate with man: *"Behold, I stand at the door, and knock: if any man hear my voice, and open the door, I will come in to him, and will sup with him, and he with me"* (Rev. 3:20).

In the other 64 books of the Bible we find God talking to man and listening for man's voice.

Psalms 50:15
And call upon me in the day of trouble: I will deliver thee, and thou shalt glorify me.

Psalms 91:15
He shall call upon me, and I will answer him: I will be with him in trouble; I will deliver him, and honour him.

Jer. 29:12
Then shall ye call upon me, and ye shall go and pray unto me, and I will hearken unto you.

Jer. 29:11-13
11 For I know the thoughts that I think toward you, saith the Lord, thoughts of peace, and not of evil, to give you an expected end.
12 Then shall ye call upon me, and ye shall go and pray unto me, and I will hearken unto you.
13 And ye shall seek me, and find me, when ye shall search for me with all your heart.

God Speaks to Us in Many Ways
We communicate with God through prayer (relationship prayer, transformation prayer and dominion prayer) as discussed in Section 1, Chapter 1. But God speaks to us in many different ways. Six of these are summarized below: (1) the written Word, (2) the preached Word, (3) the Gifts of the Spirit, (4) dreams and visions, (5) His still small Voice and (6) the massive magnificent universe. When mixed with fervent prayer we should receive greater revelation from time to time through the voice of God speaking to us in these various ways.

1. The Written Word

When our spirits are tuned to His Spirit through prayer, the Word should leap from the page and stir our hearts. Our hands should tremble when we hold God's Word because it was recorded by holy men of God as they were moved on by the Holy Ghost.

2 Peter 1:19-21
19 We have also a more sure word of prophecy; whereunto ye do well that ye take heed, as unto a light that shineth in a dark place, until the day dawn, and the day star arise in your hearts:
20 Knowing this first, that no prophecy of the Scripture is of any private interpretation.
*21 For the prophecy came not in old time by the will of man: but **holy men of God spake as they were moved by the Holy Ghost.***

The Bible is in a category of its own. It is the only Book that authenticates itself through prophecy. Critics throughout the centuries have tried to disprove it. But their theories have been discredited, and the Bible stands alone as the eternal Word of God. We should study it, memorize it, cherish it, teach it and live it.

-- From "God's Infallible Word"

According to the Bible, in the final analysis its author is God Himself. "All Scripture is given by inspiration of God" (II Timothy 3:16). In this verse, "inspiration of God" is translated from the Greek word *theopneustos*, which literally means "God-breathed." The picture is of God breathing out the words from His mouth (Matthew 4:4), creating Scripture similar to the way He created the

108

universe (Psalms 33:6). In other words, the Bible emanated from God. It is God's communication to humanity.

We can identify several characteristics of truth that are essential to its very nature; without them truth would not be truth. The Bible, as the true Word of God, necessarily exhibits these characteristics.

Absolute: not relative; not dependent on anything else; real; actual. "Let God be true but every man a liar. As it is written: That You may be justified in Your words" (Romans 3:4).

Precise: accurately stated; correct even to minute details. "Every word of God is pure" (Proverbs 30:5).

Immutable: never changing or varying; constant; stable; remaining the same. "Forever, O Lord, Your word is settled in heaven" (Psalms 119:89).

Whole: entire; complete; to be taken as a body. "You shall not add to the word which I command you, nor take anything from it" (Deuteronomy 4:2). "The law of the Lord is perfect" (Psalms 19:7).

Consistent: in agreement or harmony; in accord, unified; not contradictory. "The entirety of Your word is truth" (Psalms 119:160).

Eternal: everlasting; timeless. "The word of our God stands forever" (Isaiah 40:8). "Heaven and earth will pass away, but My words will by no means pass away" (Matthew 24:35).

Irrevocable: incapable of being withdrawn, repealed, canceled, or annulled. "Assuredly, I say to you, will heaven and earth pass away, one jot or one tittle will by no means pass from the law till all is fulfilled" (Matthew 5:18).

These points establish and underscore the infallibility of the Bible.[3]

- **The final authority is the written Word of God and although God uses other means to speak to His people no message from God will ever supersede His written Word.**

Although the Bible is a message to everyone on earth, there are individual messages and promises that provide answers and direction to our individual lives. But we will never know its power unless we read and embrace the truths locked away in its pages.

The New Testament writers stated that: *"We were eye witnesses of his majesty"*, but they could not record everything that Jesus did. The apostle John stated that the world could not contain the volumes that could have been written: *"There are also many other things which Jesus did, the which, if they should be written every one, I suppose that even the world itself could not contain the books that should be written. Amen" (John 21:25).*

From Matthew to Revelation the writers were aware of many other things that Jesus did, but when they picked up their quill to write, the Spirit moved on them what to include and exclude. God knew what we would need to get through this life to get from this world to the New Jerusalem. Every word in the Bible was recorded with us in mind.

God knew we would never master the sixty-six books that He provided, because His Word comes in layers. When we go to a new level in our relationship with God, a new level of understanding emerges from God's Word. As we pursue the study of His Word, with prayer, we receive new revelation. We may read the same passage of the Bible thirty times, but on the thirty-first reading something new emerges from its pages.

The history and stories under both the Old and New Covenants were put together with us in mind. The Bible recorded many difficult cases where God provided deliverance from trial, strength to endure and faith to prevail. God knew there would be times in our lives with deep dark valleys, difficult trials and problems. The writings in His Word record times of difficulty when God miraculously provided deliverance for people when there was no way of escape. Therefore, we need to keep the faith because we can be assured that God is the same. If He did it in the past -- He will do it today: *"Jesus Christ the same yesterday, and today, and forever" (Heb. 13:8).*

There are not many things that are stable in this world for us to depend and build our lives upon. But the Word of God is a sure foundation, a rock and an anchor for the soul: *"God also bound himself with an oath, so that those who received the promise could be perfectly sure that he would never change his mind. So God has given both his promise and his oath. These two things are unchangeable because it is impossible for God to lie. Therefore, we who have fled to him for refuge can have great confidence as we hold to the hope that lies before us. This hope is a strong and trustworthy anchor for our souls" (Heb. 6:17-19). NLT*

2. The Preached Word

Your pastor is one of the most important persons in your life, because he ministers the Word of God. God gives him insight and revelation which is imparted through teaching and preaching. Your employer provides your financial needs, and he is important. Your doctor assesses your health needs, and he is important. Your lawyer helps you with your legal needs, and he is important. But your pastor is the most important of these, because he is one of the ways that God speaks to you. He is helping you get to heaven and there is nothing else more important. When our spirits are tuned with His Spirit, the Word should leap from the pulpit to impact our lives.

Many times, I have entered the doors of the church, bruised and wounded from the burdens of life, and received a healing touch and renewed hope through the ministry of the Word. I thank God for the fivefold ministry (apostles, prophets, evangelists, pastors and teachers) that God has placed in my life for correction and instruction in righteousness.

Eph. 4:11-13
11 And he gave some, apostles; and some, prophets; and some, evangelists; and some, pastors and teachers;
12 For the perfecting of the saints, for the work of the ministry, for the edifying of the body of Christ:
13 Till we all come in the unity of the faith, and of the knowledge of the Son of God, unto a perfect man, unto the measure of the stature of the fulness of Christ:

3. The Gifts of the Spirit

It is God's will to speak to His people through the revelation gifts (the mind of Christ) and through the utterance gifts (the voice of Christ) as described in the twelfth chapter of First Corinthians. However, these supernatural gifts are given to complement and never to replace the written Word of God. The word spoken through these gifts must always be in alignment with the written Word of God because God will never declare anything contrary to His written Word.

God speaking to the church, through the Gifts of the Spirit, is a part of the apostolic ministry of the New Testament church. And hearing God's Voice in this manner is a powerful and wonderful experience that we should cherish.

4. Dreams and Visions

God speaks to us in the nighttime. He speaks to us in our subconscious mind while we sleep. Sometimes that is the only time we are quiet enough to hear His voice and listen. The word *dream* or *dreams* is used in the Bible 95 times and the word *vision* or *visions* is used 103 times. Recorded in many settings in the Old and New Testaments is God's message to man through dreams and visions: Abraham, Jacob, Joseph, Pharaoh, Solomon, Daniel, Isaiah, Ananias, Paul, Peter, etc.

Acts 2:17, 18
17 And it shall come to pass in the last days, saith God, I will pour out of my Spirit upon all flesh: and your sons and your daughters shall prophesy, and your young men shall see visions, and your old men shall dream dreams:

113

18 And on my servants and on my handmaidens I will pour out in those days of my Spirit; and they shall prophesy:

What are you dreaming? It is important what you are dreaming -- because what you are dreaming today is what you will be doing tomorrow. It is God's will for you to be filled with His Spirit; to have dreams and visions of your involvement in His Kingdom beyond what you have done in the past; and then to exercise your faith to bring the invisible into the visible and the impossible into the possible.

Vision is a picture of what you are going to be and what you are going to do for God. Vision is seeing the end from the beginning. Everything is created twice -- first in the mind and then in the real world. Vision is the object or target of faith.

"Faith is the substance of things hoped for" -- the connection between what exists today and our vision of what will be in the future.

- **Without faith, it is impossible to please God; therefore, without a vision it is impossible to have faith and please God.**

5. God's Still Small Voice

God speaks to us personally and directly at times through a still small Voice into our spirit. Hearing the voice of God is a wonderful thing, because the message is personalized just for us.

When we feel that we have heard a message from God, there may be a need for a special time of prayer and fasting to confirm it was God – that it was God's mind vs. our mind. A confirmation may come through the preached Word or from another prayerful person. But God's voice will always be in alignment with His written Word. We don't have to be super spiritual to hear God's voice. Just take time to talk to Him, and listen to Him. The more we talk to God, the more He will talk to us.

1 Kings 19:11, 12
11 And, behold, the Lord passed by, and a great and strong wind rent the mountains, and brake in pieces the rocks before the Lord; but the Lord was not in the wind: and after the wind an earthquake; but the Lord was not in the earthquake.
*12 And after the earthquake a fire; but the Lord was not in the fire: and after the fire a **still small voice**.*

6. The Massive Magnificent Universe

The greatest of God's visible supernatural acts was the creation of the magnificent and vast universe. It is so large that the astronomers refer to the part that they can see as the visible universe.

- **When God describes Himself and His greatness, He refers to the gigantic universe that He created. He declares that it was He that created the vastness and beauty of the universe, with its galaxies, solar systems and planets.**

If God places such emphasis on His creation of the sun, moon stars, the earth and the planets, possibly we should understand more about what is so great about the universe and tune our ear to the voice of God speaking from the heavens. His Word states that: *"The heavens declare the glory of God; and the firmament sheweth his handywork."*

a. At the beginning of time, in the first verse in the Bible, God declares that He created the universe - the heavens and the earth.

Gen. 1:1
In the beginning God created the Heaven and the earth.

He created heaven and earth with His spoken Word. Seven times it is recorded in the first chapter of Genesis that: *"God said let there be . . ."* and the heavens and earth were created.

b. When God spoke of His wisdom and power to Job, He spoke of His great creation:

Job 38:4-6, 8, 12, 18, 19, 31-33
4 Where were you when I laid the foundations of the earth? Tell me, if you know so much.
5 Do you know how its dimensions were determined and who did the surveying?
6 What supports its foundations, and who laid its cornerstone
8 Who defined the boundaries of the sea as it burst from the womb,
12 Have you ever commanded the morning to appear and caused the dawn to rise in the east?
18 Do you realize the extent of the earth? Tell me about it if you know!
19 Where does the light come from, and where does the darkness go?
31 Can you hold back the movements of the stars?
32 Can you ensure the proper sequence of the seasons or guide the constellation of the Bear with her cubs across the heavens?
33 Do you know the laws of the universe and how God rules the earth? NLT

c. King David continues the message of God's greatness that he observed through the vastness and magnificence of the universe.

Psalms 8:3-6, 9

3 When I consider thy heavens, the work of thy fingers, the moon and the stars, which thou hast ordained;

4 What is man, that thou art mindful of him? and the son of man, that thou visitest him?

5 For thou hast made him a little lower than the angels, and hast crowned him with glory and honour.

6 Thou madest him to have dominion over the works of thy hands; thou hast put all things under his feet:

9 O LORD our Lord, how excellent is thy name in all the earth!

Psalms 89:11, 12

11 The heavens are thine, the earth also is thine: as for the world and the fulness thereof, thou hast founded them.

12 The north and the south thou hast created them:

d. God speaks through Isaiah of His great wisdom and power shown through creation.

Isa. 40:12, 18, 21, 22, 25, 26

12 Who hath measured the waters in the hollow of his hand, and meted out heaven with the span,

18 To whom then will ye liken God? or what likeness will ye compare unto him?

21 Have ye not known? have ye not heard? hath it not been told you from the beginning? have ye not understood from the foundations of the earth?

22 It is he that sitteth upon the circle of the earth, and the inhabitants thereof are as grasshoppers; that stretcheth out the heavens as a curtain, and spreadeth them out as a tent to dwell in:

117

25 To whom then will ye liken me, or shall I be equal? saith he Holy One.
26 Lift up your eyes on high, and behold who hath created these things, that bringeth out their host by number: he calleth them all by names by the greatness of his might.

Isa. 45:5-7
5 I am the LORD, and there is none else, there is no God beside me:
6 That they may know from the rising of the sun, and from the west, that there is none beside me. I am the LORD, and there is none else.
7 I form the light, and create darkness: . . . I the LORD do all these things.

Our Incredible Universe Speaks of an Infinite God

The size and power of God can be seen in the gigantic universe that He created. When He said: **"Let there be light and there was light"**, it started across the heavens at 186,000 miles per second, 11,000,000 per minute, 660,000,000 miles per hour. The universe is so vast that it is measured in light years -- how far light can travel in one year. The known universe is 14 billion light years across! The known universe has 350 billion large galaxies, 3.5 trillion small galaxies and 30 billion, trillion stars.

Our galaxy alone (the Milky Way, the sub-division in which we live) is 100,000 light years in diameter has been estimated to contain more than a hundred billion stars and a trillion solar masses. It is one of tens of millions of galaxies known to man. Our solar system (a small part of the Milky Way) consists of the earth and the other planets that are subject to the gravitation pull of the sun.

118

- **The perfection and timing of our solar system (a tiny part of the universe) proves that there is a powerful God that created this and keeps it all in balance.**

I will debate anyone that doesn't believe in God based on the following four facts concerning the movement and the perfect timing of the sun, earth and moon in our solar system.

a. The Timing of One Day

The length of one day is 24 hours. The earth rotates at the rate of 1,100 miles per hour. It is 27,000 miles around the circumference of the earth. The length of one day is always exactly 24 hours which is one complete rotation of the earth. It is day when the earth faces the sun and night when the earth faces away from the sun.

You have never heard a newscaster announce: "Warning, reset your clocks. Today will be a little longer because there has been a slight variation in the speed of the earth's rotation." But since the beginning of time, when God set the earth in motion, the timing of one day has remained constant. God's timing pieces for the day and night are more accurate than man's computers and technology -- man resets his clock by God's clock.

Gen. 1:14
And God said, Let there be lights in the firmament of the heaven to divide the day from the night; and let them be for signs, and for seasons, and for days, and years.

b. The Timing of One Year

The length of one year is 365.25 days. The earth is hurling through space at a rate of 67,000 miles per hour on a 579,000,000 mile orbit around the sun.

The length of one year is exactly 365.25 days, the time it takes for the earth to make one trip in its orbit around the sun. The timing of the earth's 579,000,000 mile annual trip around the sun is never off one day. You have never heard a newscaster announce: "Warning, reset your calendars. This year will be a little longer because there has been a slight variation in the speed of the earth's trip around the sun." But since the beginning of time, when God set the earth in motion, the timing for a year has remained constant.

c. The Timing of the Sun's Movement
The sun is moving through the Milky Way Galaxy at the rate of 486,000 miles per hour. It takes 226 million years for the sun to make one trip around the Milky Way Galaxy. For the earth to stay in a fixed orbit around the sun, it must move in a third dimension at the same speed -- in effect chasing the sun.

d. The Timing of the Moon Orbiting the Earth
The moon rotates around the earth once every 27.322 days. Amazingly the moon also makes one revolution on its axis every 27.322 days. The term the "far-side" of the moon refers to the fact that the same side of the moon always faces the earth. In other words, it takes the same amount of time for the moon to rotate once as it does for the moon to orbit the earth once. Therefore, earth-bound observers can never see the "far-side" of the moon.

The perfection of the moon's movement around the earth allows man to predict the following events, years in advance:

- The phases of the moon (new moon, waxing crescent, first quarter, waxing gibbous, full moon, waning gibbous, last quarter, waning crescent). This cycle is completed every 27.322 days.
- The cycle of two high tides and two low tides, which occurs on the coastlines of the world each day.

Summary of the Earth's Three-Dimensional Movement

	Speed	**Distance**	**Time**
a.	1,100 mph Revolving on its axis	27,000 miles	24 hours (1 day)
b.	67,000 mph Revolving around the sun	570,000,000 miles	365.25 days (1 year)
c.	486,000 mph Moving through the Milky Way	962,822,376,000,000,000 miles	226,000,000 Years

When we consider the mind-boggling, magnificent timing and speed of the earth's movement, hurling through space in three dimensions, we must bow low and exclaim: *"Oh Lord, our Lord, how excellent is Thy name in all the earth -- the heavens declare your glory."*

There are many other aspects of our solar system, such as: what causes the seasons, and how life is sustained on earth with the delicate balance of temperature and oxygen, etc. These will not be discussed here but are discussed in more details in Volume IV, "Unlimited Partnership with a Supernatural God."

121

- **If God declares His greatness by referring to His creation of the vast and incomprehensible universe, should we not do the same? We should recognize and declare every day:** *"Oh Lord, our Lord, how excellent is thy name in all the earth -- the heavens declare your glory."*

Our great infinite, omnipotent and supernatural God, who controls the vast universe, comes down to our level and ministers to our individual needs.

On one hand our great supernatural God, who is a billion, trillion times larger than the universe, rules high above over the vast expanse of the heavens. But on the other hand, He comes down to our level and involves Himself in our individual affairs.

God is so big that the universe cannot hold Him, but He came to a tiny spec in the universe called the Milky Way (our galaxy) and then to a tiny spec in the Milky Way called earth. He came down further to the tiny town of Bethlehem and down further to a cold, dirty animal stable to be born in the most humble and uncomfortable setting.

Why did He do this? It was because He loved us and wanted to have a relationship with man that would listen and talk to Him. Out of all the people on the earth, each of us is just a grain of sand on the shores of time. But our measureless, infinite, omnipotent, omnipresent, omniscient, supernatural God knows each of us intimately and ministers to our individual needs.

- **Notice the contrast in the following Scriptures. In one Scripture God is ministering to man's individual needs and in the very next Scripture He is working at the vast universe level.**

Psalms 147:3, 4
3 He healeth the broken in heart, and bindeth up their wounds.
{personal level}
4 He telleth the number of the stars, he calleth them all by their names. **{universe level}**

Isa. 40:11, 12, 22
11 He will feed his flock like a shepherd: he will gather the lambs with his arm, and carry them in his bosom; he will gently lead them. **{personal level}**
12 Who hath measured the waters in the hollow of his hand, and meted out the heavens with the span,
22 [It is] he that sitteth upon the circle of the earth, and stretcheth out the heavens as a curtain. **{universe level}**

It is an invaluable privilege to have an audience with the Creator of the universe. We should never take for granted the privilege to have an individual audience with the supernatural, all powerful, infinite King of kings and Lord of lords. To have His attention when we talk to Him in prayer and to hear Him speak to us is the most valuable gift we could ever possess.

Important and famous people don't have much time, if any, for the average man. Doctors are rushed with their business and give us very little of their time. Specialists and surgeons are very protective of their time. No doctor, lawyer or consultant can give us unlimited time and attention and if they would, we could not afford it.

123

But we can schedule an appointment with the Creator of the universe at any time of the day or night for an unlimited amount of time. His line is never busy. His calendar is not full. There is no waiting -- no waiting room. He is not rushed. We can talk to Him as long as we like -- asking and telling Him anything. And when the appointment is over, we will feel so much better -- knowing He has heard us and will do what is best for us.

The Creator's Invitation

Mark 11:24
Therefore I say unto you, What things soever ye desire, when ye pray, believe that ye receive them, and ye shall have them.

Luke 11:9
And I say unto you, Ask, and it shall be given you; seek, and ye shall find; knock, and it shall be opened unto you.

1 John 5:14, 15
14 And this is the confidence that we have in him, that, if we ask any thing according to his will, he heareth us:
15 And if we know that he hear us, whatsoever we ask, we know that we have the petitions that we desired of him.

Acts 17:27, 28
27 That they should seek the Lord, if haply they might feel after him, and find him, though he be not far from every one of us:
28 For in him we live, and move, and have our being

Heb. 4:16
Let us therefore come boldly unto the throne of grace, that we may obtain mercy, and find grace to help in time of need.

Deut. 4:29
But if from thence thou shalt seek the Lord thy God, thou shalt find him, if thou seek him with all thy heart and with all thy soul.

Psalms 34:15
The eyes of the LORD are upon the righteous, and his ears are open unto their cry.

Psalms 50:15
And call upon me in the day of trouble: I will deliver thee, and thou shalt glorify me.

Psalms 91:15
He shall call upon me, and I will answer him: I will be with him in trouble; I will deliver him, and honour him.

Isa. 58:9
Then shalt thou call, and the Lord shall answer; thou shalt cry, and he shall say, Here I am.

Isa. 65:24
And it shall come to pass, that before they call, I will answer; and while they are yet speaking, I will hear.

Jer. 33:3
Call unto me, and I will answer thee, and shew thee great and mighty things, which thou knowest not.

"Ye have not chosen me, but I have chosen you, and ordained you, that ye should go and bring forth fruit, and that your fruit should remain." (John 15:16)

* * * * *

"But ye shall receive power, after that the Holy Ghost is come upon you: and ye shall be witnesses unto me both in Jerusalem, and in all Judaea, and in Samaria, and unto the uttermost part of the earth." (Acts 1:8)

2. God Works Through Man to Perform His Will on Earth

From the beginning of time, God's purpose for creating man included **relationship;** however, it was much more than that. It was to establish a partnership with Himself, and give man **dominion** to carry out His mission, His will and His work on earth. Dominion means to prevail against, to reign, to rule in a kingdom or a domain.

There is the kingdom of this world and there is the Kingdom of God. It is God's plan for us, His children, to prevail against His enemies -- the kingdom of this world, the god of this world, Satan. It is God's will for us to work and partner with Him in His domain – exercising dominion in His Kingdom business.

- **How effective we are in our dominion role is dependent on our connection with God through effectual, fervent prayer.**

James 5:16
*The earnest prayer of a righteous man has **great power and wonderful results**. TLB*

Mark 16:20
*And they went forth, and preached everywhere, **the Lord working with them, and confirming the word** with signs following. Amen.*

If we are going to rule and reign with Him on this earth in the "by and by", then we must rule and reign with Him in the "here and now".

Rev. 20:6
*Blessed and holy is he that hath part in the first resurrection: on such the second death hath no power, but they shall be priests of God and of Christ, **and shall reign with Him a thousand years.***

-- From "E. M. Bounds on Prayer"

The prayers of God's saints are the capital stock in heaven by which Christ carries on His great work upon the earth. The earth is changed, revolutionized; angels move on more powerful, more rapid wings; and God's policy is shaped when the prayers of His people are more numerous and more efficient.

When God's house on the earth is a house of prayer, then God's house in heaven is busy and powerful in its plans and movements. *'For mine house shall be called an house of prayer for all people'* (Isa. 56:7), says our God. Then, His earthly armies are clothed with the triumphs and spoils of victory, and His enemies are defeated on every hand.

God shapes the world by prayer. The more praying there is in the world, the better the world will be and the mightier the forces against evil everywhere. The very life and prosperity of God's cause -- even its very existence -- depend on prayer.[1]

God's plan has never changed. Man was made to rule the earth for God -- to have dominion, authority and power. He was to reflect the glory of God, revealing God to those who did not know Him. He said, "Adam, you have dominion. You are in charge of My mission, My purpose, My will, and My work on earth."

God's decision to do nothing on earth except through man is a wonderful truth. In making this choice, God placed Himself in a relationship that He would need man to carry out His work and will. God needs man; man needs God. Those who say God doesn't need you or me, don't understand the key principle of relationship. And that is, both parties must have a mutual need and a dependence on one another. Otherwise, it is one-sided and not a valid relationship or contract.

I can rejoice in the fact that God needs me and depends on me to carry on His work. And, oh God, I need You. I need Your help and wisdom to work out impossible situations and problems in my life that I could never solve in a lifetime.

- **God created this earth and He owns it, but He has assigned it to man to govern and rule. He has chosen man to be the intercessor here, to carry on His work, His will and purpose.**

Psalms 115:16
16 The heaven, even the heavens, are the LORD's: **but the earth hath He given to the children of men.**

16 The heavens belong to the Lord, **but He has given the earth to all mankind.** *TLB*

16 ..... the earth He has assigned to men. MOF

The Vital Importance of Prayer

God has put man in charge on earth, for God, with God and under God. God created man in His image because He wanted a son who would:

- Think like Him.
- Love what He loves.
- Hate what He hates.
- Do His will.
- Carry on His mission and business on earth.

He assigned man to govern the earth. Man is God's intercessor in the battle against God's enemies and in the harvest to seek and save the lost.

God made Adam in His image, He put His breath in him, He put His glory on him, and then He told him: "I am giving you dominion. You are in charge. You are My agent to carry out My mission and work on earth. You are My hands, My feet, My eyes, My ears, and My mouthpiece on the earth." King David declared this awesome concept in his writings:

Psalms 8:3-6
3 When I consider thy heavens, the work of thy fingers, the moon and the stars, which thou hast ordained;
4 What is man, that thou art mindful of him? and the son of man, that thou visitest him?
*5 For thou hast made him a **little lower than the angels,** and hast crowned him with glory and honor.*
*6 Thou madest him to have **dominion** over the works of thy hands; thou hast **put all things under his feet:***

-- From "Theological Wordbook of the Old Testament"

"than the angels" (Strong's Greek Hebrew number 430) 'elohiym; plural of OT:433; gods in the ordinary sense; but specifically used (in the plural thus, especially with the article) of the supreme God.[2]

Psalms 8:5 (Man was made a little lower than deity.)
5 For thou hast made him but little lower than God, and crownest him with glory and honor. ASV

5 Yet you made him inferior only to yourself; you crowned him with glory and honor. TEV

Man is much more valuable to God than angels. When the angels committed one sin, God did not lift a finger to recover or save them. He cast them out of heaven to be doomed forever. But when one man, Adam, sinned, God promised that He would come to earth and die for mankind so that they could be forgiven and saved.

Jude 6
And the angels which kept not their first estate, but left their own habitation, He hath reserved in everlasting chains under darkness unto the judgment of the great day.

Man is a beloved son of God. In the New Testament we are His bride, His love. He loved us so much that He suffered, bled and died for us. God needs us and we surely need Him. This is a great partnership and a great relationship.

God's purpose for creating man in the beginning and His purpose for the New Testament church are the same: Relationship and Dominion.

Apostle Paul's writings in Ephesians 4:11, 12 identify the same two purposes for which Jesus created the New Testament church to:

1. Perfect the saints (Relationship)

2. Equip the saints for the work of the ministry (Dominion)

131

Eph. 4:11, 12
11 And He gave some, apostles; and some, prophets; and some, evangelists; and some, pastors and teachers;
*12 For the (1) **Perfecting of the saints**, (2) For the **work of the ministry**, for the edifying of the body of Christ:*

*12 **To prepare God's people for works of service**, so that the body of Christ may be built up.   NIV*

*12 **For the equipping of the saints for the work of service.** NASU*

This speaks of dominion to complete the mission and work that Jesus started and exampled on earth for three and one-half years. Jesus said that His purpose and mission for coming to this world involved two things:

- Destroying the works of the devil. (John 3:8)
- Seeking and saving the lost. (Luke 19:10)

We have well accepted **relationship** as the purpose for which God created man. Relationship with God brings the blessings of God in our lives. But we have understood less about the second purpose of **dominion** -- to carry out His will and work on earth.

While relationship brings God's blessings; fulfilling the role of dominion brings His favor. Everyone wants to be in relationship with God to receive His blessings, but fulfilling the dominion role as a son of God is also a part of His eternal purpose and will for man.

The importance of dominion is emphasized in the teachings of Jesus:

1. Jesus was asked: *"Which is the greatest commandment?"* His answer:

- *Love the Lord thy God with all thy heart, and with all thy soul, and with all thy mind.* (**Relationship** with God).

- *Love thy neighbor as thyself.* (**Dominion** - carrying out God's mission by ministering to the needs of your neighbor). Jesus in the parable of the Good Samaritan defined our neighbor as anyone in need.

2. In the parable of the talents given to the servants (Matt. 25:14-30), when the master returned from a long journey, he demanded an accounting of what they had done with his resources. Those who gained additional talents were commended by the master. The servant who maintained only his original talent was cast into outer darkness.

3. The all-consuming priority of Jesus (dominion) is obvious in His last commandment before He left the earth and His first question to be asked at the Judgment:

a. The **last commandment** of Jesus before He left this earth was: **"Go"**. Known as the Great Commission, this was recorded in the first five books of the New Testament.

b. The **first question to be asked at the Judgment: "Did you go? Did you minister to those in need** -- the hungry, thirsty, stranger, naked, sick, and those in prison?" (Matt. 26:31-46)

God's promise for rain in Israel was fulfilled through Elijah's intercessory prayers

Because of Israel's and King Ahab's sin, it had not rained in Israel for three years. When it became God's will to send rain, He told the prophet Elijah to inform the king. Although the prophecy was given, there was no sign of rain.

1 Kings 18:42-44
42 Elijah went up to the top of Carmel; and he cast himself down upon the earth, and put his face between his knees.
43 And said to his servant, Go up now, look toward the sea. And he went up, and looked, and said, There is nothing. And he said, Go again seven times.
44 And it came to pass at the seventh time, that he said, Behold, there ariseth a little cloud out of the sea, like a man's hand. And he said, Go up, say unto Ahab, Prepare thy chariot, and get thee down, that the rain stop thee not.

It did not rain until Elijah climbed to the mountaintop to pray into fulfillment the promise of God. Elijah travailed in prayer as he put his head between his knees (the childbearing position in some cultures). He spent several hours interceding in prayer as his servant checked seven times for a sign of rain.

God's promise for the restoration of Israel to their homeland was fulfilled through Daniel's prayers

Daniel knew much about prayer. He prayed three times a day, even when his life was threatened for doing so. He is the only person in the Bible where it is recorded that both Gabriel and Michael, the archangels, got involved in bringing answers to his intercessory prayers.

Israel had been in Babylonian captivity for many years. One

134

day in Daniel's devotion, he read in Jeremiah that the nation of Israel would be restored to their homeland after 70 years. Daniel realized that this time period had already elapsed.

Dan. 9:2-4
2 In that first year of his reign, I, Daniel, learned from the book of Jeremiah the prophet, that Jerusalem must lie desolate for seventy years.
3 So I earnestly pleaded with the Lord God [to end our captivity and send us back to our own land]. As I prayed, I fasted and wore rough sackcloth, and I sprinkled myself with ashes.
4 And confessed my sins and those of my people. "O Lord," I prayed, "you are a great and awesome God; you always fulfill your promises of mercy to those who love you and keep your laws." TLB

Seventy years had expired and they were still in captivity. There was nothing happening that resembled deliverance from Babylon. As Daniel began to understand the prophecy of restoration, he sought the Lord through prayer and supplication with fasting in humility of sackcloth and ashes. He repented for Israel's sins and disobedience. Daniel's burden and intercessory prayer started the wheels rolling for Israel's prophesied restoration to their homeland.

God's promise for the restoration of the endtime church will be fulfilled by our prayers and actions.

There are times when a prophecy has not been fulfilled because it is not yet God's time. The calendar and endtime prophecy indicate we are living at the very end of the 2,000 year Church Age -- the midnight hour preceding the coming of Jesus Christ. The complete restoration of apostolic ministry with signs, wonders and miracles will be realized when we pray into fulfillment the prophecies and promises of God's Word.

It is the Endtime -- Time for the Completion of Restoration

God created the world in six days and rested on the seventh (the Sabbath). He set in motion 6,000 years as the period for man's day. Approximately 4,000 years (four great days) passed before God robed Himself in flesh; walked on this earth for 33 years; suffered and died for our sins; and then ascended into heaven. Approximately 2,000 years (two great days), since the birth of the church on the Day of Pentecost have elapsed. We now stand at the end of the sixth day -- at the week's end of human history. The morning of the seventh day will break upon a new millennia:

- Millennial Reign of Jesus Christ.
- A thousand years of peace.
- Sabbath of the World.
- Restoration of the earth to the Garden of Eden state.

Jesus Christ came to this world, ascended into heaven and He will return when restoration is complete -- "the restitution of all things":

Acts 3:20, 21
20 And he shall send Jesus Christ, which before was preached unto you:
*21 Whom the heaven must receive **until the times of restitution of all things**, which God hath spoken by the mouth of all his holy prophets since the world began.*

21 Whom heaven must receive [and retain] **until the time for the complete restoration** *of all that God spoke by the mouth of all His holy prophets for ages past [from the most ancient time in the memory of man].* *AMP*

21 For the time being he must remain out of sight in heaven until **everything is restored to order** *again just the way God, through the preaching of his holy prophets of old, said it would be.* *MSG*

It is God's will for us to be a part of the restoration of His church, involving ourselves in a dominion role in this last day harvest – driven by effectual fervent prayer. We must be willing to go into new places in the Spirit beyond where we have ever been. We must:

1. Be led and empowered by the Spirit.
2. Elevate God and His business to the highest priority until it becomes our chief joy.
3. Claim the prophecies for restoration of the endtime church with intercessory prayer.

1. We must be led and empowered by the Spirit.

To be led by the Spirit we must allow the Spirit to:

- Be preeminent (number one) in our lives through a **closer relationship** with God.

- **Transform** our lives: *"Be ye transformed by the renewing of your mind, that ye may prove what is that good, and acceptable, and perfect, will of God."*

- Lead us into a **greater dominion role** in doing God's will and work.

137

God only claims us as His sons if we allow His Spirit to lead us. The Spirit will always take us further into His purpose, will and work.

Rom. 8:14
*For as many as are **led by the Spirit of God**, they are the sons of God.*

Gal. 5:25
*If we are living now by the Holy Spirit's power, let us **follow the Holy Spirit's leading in every part of our lives.*** TLB*

As we are led by the Spirit, we will be sent to fulfill the mission that Jesus Christ began in His earthly ministry and declared in His first sermon text from Isaiah 61:1 (recorded in Luke 4:18). When the Spirit sends us, He will also anoint us with divine ability to do His will. Like Jesus, we will be anointed and sent.

Luke 4:18, 19
*18 The Spirit of the Lord is upon me, because he hath **anointed me** to preach the gospel to the poor; he hath **sent me** to heal the brokenhearted, to preach deliverance to the captives, and recovering of sight to the blind, to set at liberty them that are bruised,*
19 To preach the acceptable year of the Lord.

Restoration is all about the working of God's Spirit through His church and His people (as sons of God) with miracles, signs and wonders, to confirm the Word and reach lost souls. When God partners with man in His supernatural work, He bypasses man's natural abilities. His Spirit resident in the believer accomplishes the supernatural work. Apostle Paul declares: *"I can do all things through Christ which strengtheneth me"*. The Old Testament prophet Zechariah declared a timeless truth when he said: *"Not by might, nor by power, but by my spirit, saith the Lord of hosts."*

Refer to the PowerPoint charts at the end of this chapter which highlight the key element of prayer in God's divine ability working through man to perform His supernatural acts.

2. We must elevate God and His business to the highest priority in our lives until it becomes our chief joy.

Something in the heart of most Jewish people is not complete outside the Promised Land. Likewise, the Kingdom of God must occupy the highest position and priority in our lives. It must be our greatest joy -- **our chief joy.**

King David, the man after God's own heart, penned an eternal truth that remains after three millennia: Jerusalem, Zion, His Kingdom should be our highest priority and chief joy.

King David is referring to a time when the Israelites were prisoners of war in Babylon. They were captives far away from their homeland seemingly with no possibility of returning.

Psalms 137:1, 5, 6
1 By the rivers of Babylon, there we sat down, yea, we wept, when we remembered Zion.
5 If I forget you, O Jerusalem, let my right hand forget its skill [with the harp].
*6 Let my tongue cleave to the roof of my mouth if I remember you not, if **I prefer not Jerusalem above my chief joy!** AMP*

Psalms 137:5, 6
5 If I forget you, O Jerusalem, let my right hand forget its skill upon the harp.

139

*6 If I fail to **love her more than my highest joy**, let me never sing again. TLB*

-- From "Barnes' Notes"

[If I prefer not Jerusalem] literally, "If I do not cause to ascend." That is, if I do not exalt Jerusalem in my estimation above everything that gives me pleasure; if I do not find my supreme happiness in that.

[Above my chief joy] The chief thing which gives me joy; as the head is the chief, or is supreme over the body. There are other sources of joy which are not in any way inconsistent with the Kingdom of God: the joy of friendship; of domestic life; of honorable pursuits of the esteem of people. So of music, the arts, gardens, literature, science. But when one interferes with the other, or is inconsistent with the other, the joy of the world is to be sacrificed to the joy of God's Kingdom. When the joy of God's Kingdom is sacrificed for the joy of the world, it proves that there is no true devotion in the soul. The Kingdom of God must always be supreme.[3]

- **Jerusalem or Zion to us in the New Testament church is the Kingdom of God and it must always be our first priority -- our chief joy.**

- **Only strong Christians will experience the completed work of restoration. To be strong Christians, we must be joyful because, *"The joy of the Lord is our strength" (Neh. 8:10).***

- **When the work and will of God become our chief joy, it will occupy the highest priority in our lives -- positioning us to partner with Him in the supernatural.**

Our Father's business is unlike any other. His business enterprise surpasses all others. There is no comparison to another, because His Kingdom is on a different plane. The Kingdom of God, to which every believer is a part, holds a place in time and importance that every other kingdom, past, present, and future pales in comparison.

We should determine that we will stand at the Judgment having been more dedicated to the Father's business than we were to the business of our kingdom. May we have the testimony of apostle Paul, before his execution in a Roman prison: I have given my best to the Father's business: *"For I am already being poured out like a drink offering . . . I have fought the good fight, I have finished the race, I have kept the faith" (2 Tim. 4:6) NIV.* His entire life had been poured out for the sake of Christ, now he is giving his life -- giving it all.

3. We must claim the prophecies for restoration of the endtime church with intercessory prayer.

The simple requirement for the church to be restored is for born-again Christians to become book of Acts Christians. This is a continuous process -- pursuing our dominion role and becoming partakers of His divine nature.
- Spiritual growth at the individual level will result in church growth at the corporate level.
- Evangelism at the personal level will result in evangelism at the corporate level.

"The Word of God gives a promise that the latter house will be greater than the former. The former house is the early church which is our pattern for restoration. And according to His promise, the restoration of the "temple made without hands" that the Lord has allowed us to build, will be built. Jesus is the Master Builder and we are the workmen.

If He will not use us, He will use others but it will be built and restored to its former glory. The Old Testament history of the restoration of the temple at Jerusalem is given as an example for us, a blueprint and plumb line."[4]

The choice is ours today -- the last days before the coming of Jesus Christ:

- We can become satisfied with the status quo and fail to be a part of what God is doing in the restoration of His church,

- Or, we can urgently and passionately pursue a deeper relationship with God and become a book of Acts Christian -- significantly affecting our lost world with God's supernatural power working in us and through us.

Pursuing the path of restoration and a book of Acts Christian may not be an issue affecting our salvation, but it is for our lost world. If we fall short of God's plan of restoration, precious souls will be lost.

The last day church, just before the coming of Jesus Christ, will not be weak and ineffective in a survival mode. But God's promise of restoration will be fulfilled. His church will be at the zenith of its power and glory involved in revival and evangelism -- with miracles and signs exceeding that of the first century church. If we diligently desire and pursue the will of God, we can be a part of God's supernatural work in the endtime.

Jesus Christ is coming back after a powerfully restored church: a holy church, a glorious church, a church with saints demonstrating the supernatural power of its Master Designer and Builder – Jesus Christ.

Eph. 5:25-27
25 Christ also loved the church, and gave himself for it;
26 That he might sanctify and cleanse it with the washing of water by the word,
*27 **That he might present it to himself a glorious church**, not having spot, or wrinkle, or any such thing; but that it should be holy and without blemish.*

- **May all of us as born-again believers pursue our God-called dominion role through prayer. And for the rest of our lifetime may we devote ourselves to searching out and doing God's will -- that in our lives, God's will may be done on earth as it is in heaven.**

143

The Vital Importance of Prayer

Refer to the following pages for these PowerPoint charts:

Chart	Chart Name and Comments
R-1	**What Hinders Restoration and Revival -- Flow to Vs. Flow Through** It is not: God, or that it is not time, or the devil, or that there are not enough sinners. It is simply that the veil of self (our will, mind, emotions) must be broken to allow God's supernatural power to flow unrestrained through our lives to meet the needs of lost souls.
R-2	**He is the Vine and we are the Branches** The gifts of the Spirit flow through the charity channel, from the vine through the branch, to produce fruit (meeting the needs of healing, deliverance and salvation).
R-3	**The Path to the Supernatural for the Christian** He must increase and I must decrease. Less of my will, mind and emotions and more of God's will, mind and agape love.
R-4	**The Path to the Dominion in the Supernatural Through the Core Ministry of the Church** Man's natural talents are used and anointed by God to perform the supporting helps and ministries of the church. But when God performs His supernatural work, it is His divine ability that works through supernatural gifts, bypassing man's natural abilities.
R-5	**Impartation + Encounter and Engagement with Satan and Sickness Releases Supernatural Power** Jesus went into the wilderness full of the Spirit where He encountered and overcame the forces of Satan. He came out of the wilderness in the power of the Spirit and His miracle ministry began. (Luke 4:1-14)
R-6	**Using our Dual Nature as Son of God and Son of Man** Ministering to physical needs first as son of man, then spiritual needs as a son of God.
R-7	**The Soul Winning Life Cycle** (1) Building a relationship with God, (2) Building a relationship with man (son of man), (3) Ministering to spiritual needs as a son God.

144

Chart R-1

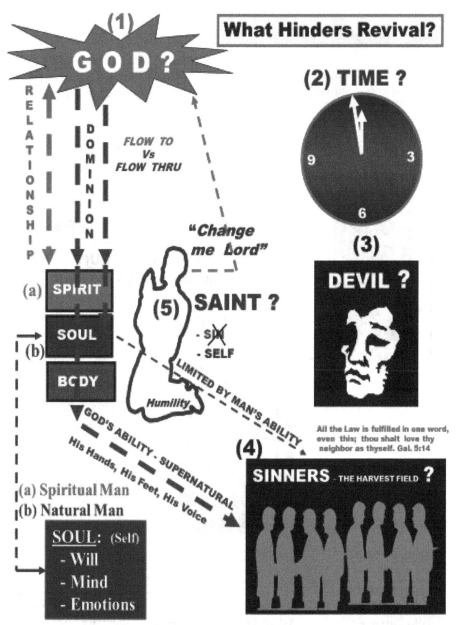

The Greatest Hindrance to Revival is Lack of Dominion Over Self (relying on our natural talents Vs. the Spirit).

Chart R-2

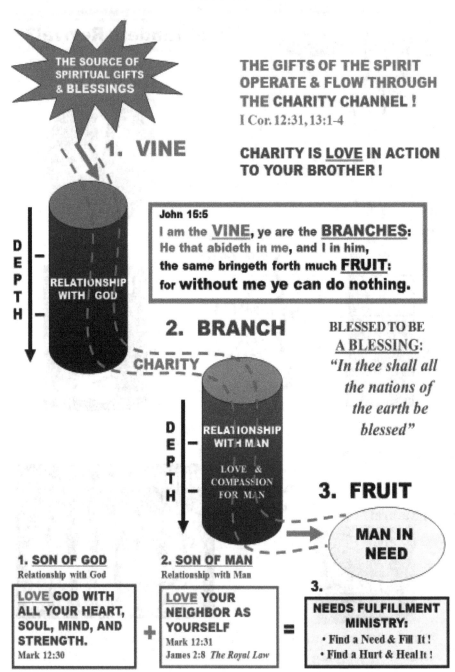

THE SOURCE OF SPIRITUAL GIFTS & BLESSINGS

THE GIFTS OF THE SPIRIT OPERATE & FLOW THROUGH THE CHARITY CHANNEL !
I Cor. 12:31, 13:1-4

1. VINE

CHARITY IS **LOVE** IN ACTION TO YOUR BROTHER !

John 15:5
I am the **VINE**, ye are the **BRANCHES**: He that abideth in me, and I in him, the same bringeth forth much **FRUIT**: for **without me ye can do nothing.**

DEPTH

RELATIONSHIP WITH GOD

2. BRANCH

CHARITY

BLESSED TO BE A BLESSING: *"In thee shall all the nations of the earth be blessed"*

DEPTH

RELATIONSHIP WITH MAN

LOVE & COMPASSION FOR MAN

3. FRUIT

MAN IN NEED

1. SON OF GOD
Relationship with God

LOVE GOD WITH ALL YOUR HEART, SOUL, MIND, AND STRENGTH.
Mark 12:30

+

2. SON OF MAN
Relationship with Man

LOVE YOUR NEIGHBOR AS YOURSELF
Mark 12:31
James 2:8 *The Royal Law*

=

3.

NEEDS FULFILLMENT MINISTRY:
• Find a Need & Fill It !
• Find a Hurt & Heal It !

Chart R-3

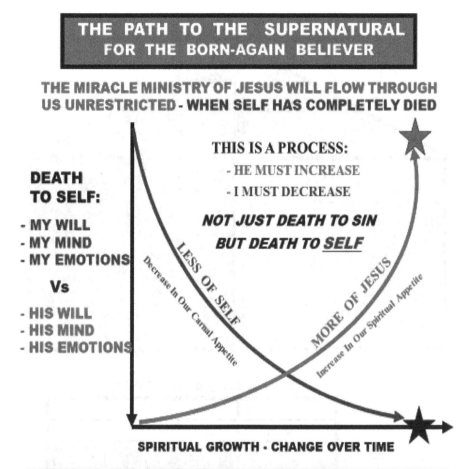

THE PATH TO THE SUPERNATURAL FOR THE BORN-AGAIN BELIEVER

THE MIRACLE MINISTRY OF JESUS WILL FLOW THROUGH US UNRESTRICTED - WHEN SELF HAS COMPLETELY DIED

DEATH TO SELF:

- MY WILL
- MY MIND
- MY EMOTIONS

Vs

- HIS WILL
- HIS MIND
- HIS EMOTIONS

THIS IS A PROCESS:
- HE MUST INCREASE
- I MUST DECREASE

NOT JUST DEATH TO SIN BUT DEATH TO SELF

LESS OF SELF — Decrease In Our Carnal Appetite

MORE OF JESUS — Increase In Our Spiritual Appetite

SPIRITUAL GROWTH - CHANGE OVER TIME

IN THE NEW TESTAMENT: (Why did John the Baptist have to die?)
John the Baptist was the forerunner of Jesus' miracle ministry. His message of "He must increase, but I must decrease", was a self-fulfilled prophecy when he was imprisoned, and put to death as the miracle ministry of Jesus began.

IN THE OLD TESTAMENT: (Why did Jonathan have to die?)
Saul is a type of the flesh. Jonathan is a type of the soul (self - the will, the mind, and the emotions). David is a type of the Spirit. Both Saul and Jonathan had to die before David could come to the throne.

Chart R-4

THE PATH TO DOMINION IN THE SUPERNATURAL
Through the Core Ministry of the Church
The Only Hope For Reaching This Lost End-time Generation

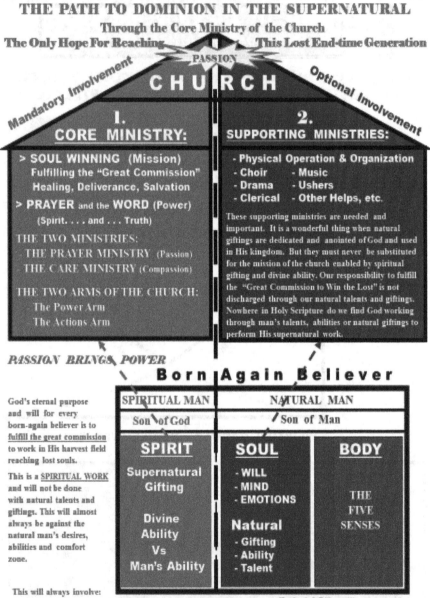

PASSION

Mandatory Involvement

Optional Involvement

CHURCH

1. CORE MINISTRY:

> **SOUL WINNING** (Mission)
  Fulfilling the "Great Commission"
  Healing, Deliverance, Salvation

> **PRAYER** and the **WORD** (Power)
  (Spirit. . . . and . . . Truth)

THE TWO MINISTRIES:
  THE PRAYER MINISTRY (Passion)
  THE CARE MINISTRY (Compassion)

THE TWO ARMS OF THE CHURCH:
  The Power Arm
  The Actions Arm

2. SUPPORTING MINISTRIES:

- Physical Operation & Organization
- Choir   - Music
- Drama   - Ushers
- Clerical   - Other Helps, etc.

These supporting ministries are needed and
important. It is a wonderful thing when natural
giftings are dedicated and anointed of God and used
in His kingdom. But they must never be substituted
for the mission of the church enabled by spiritual
gifting and divine ability. Our responsibility to fulfill
the "Great Commission to Win the Lost" is not
discharged through our natural talents and giftings.
Nowhere in Holy Scripture do we find God working
through man's talents, abilities or natural giftings to
perform His supernatural work.

PASSION BRINGS POWER

Born Again Believer

God's eternal purpose
and will for every
born-again believer is to
fulfill the great commission
to work in His harvest field
reaching lost souls.

This is a SPIRITUAL WORK
and will not be done
with natural talents and
giftings. This will almost
always be against the
natural man's desires,
abilities and comfort
zone.

SPIRITUAL MAN	NATURAL MAN	
Son of God	Son of Man	
SPIRIT	**SOUL**	**BODY**
Supernatural Gifting	- WILL - MIND - EMOTIONS	THE FIVE SENSES
Divine Ability Vs Man's Ability	Natural - Gifting - Ability - Talent	

This will always involve:
 - His Will Vs Our Will (Not Our Choice but His)
 - His Thinking Vs Our Thinking (His ways)
 - His Emotions Vs Our Emotions (Deep sorrow
   for their suffering with a strong urge to help)

Power

*Zech. 4:6-7 You will not succeed by
your own strength, but by my Spirit.
Obstacles as great as mountains will
disappear before you. TEV*

Chart R-5

Impartation + Encounter and Engagement with the Forces of Satan and Sickness Releases Supernatural Power!

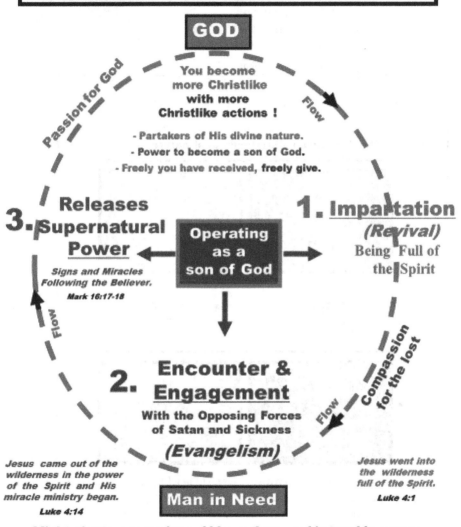

GOD

You become more Christlike with more Christlike actions !

- Partakers of His divine nature.
- Power to become a son of God.
- Freely you have received, **freely give.**

Passion for God

Flow

3. Releases Supernatural Power

Signs and Miracles Following the Believer.

Mark 16:17-18

Flow

Operating as a son of God

1. Impartation

(Revival)

Being Full of the Spirit

Compassion for the lost

Flow

2. Encounter & Engagement

With the Opposing Forces of Satan and Sickness

(Evangelism)

Jesus came out of the wilderness in the power of the Spirit and His miracle ministry began.

Luke 4:14

Jesus went into the wilderness full of the Spirit.

Luke 4:1

Man in Need

Ministering to someone in need blesses them - and in turn blesses you.

149

Chart R-6

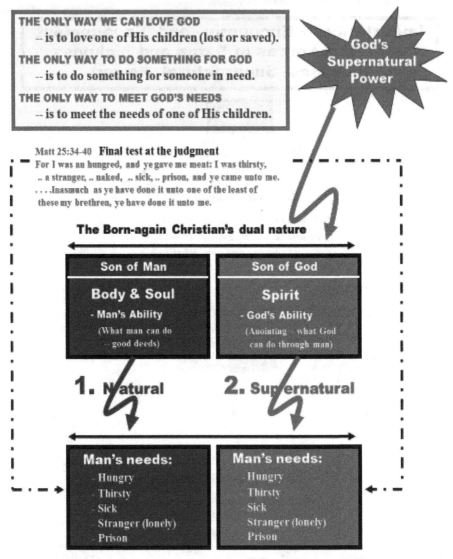

THE ONLY WAY WE CAN LOVE GOD
-- is to love one of His children (lost or saved).

THE ONLY WAY TO DO SOMETHING FOR GOD
-- is to do something for someone in need.

THE ONLY WAY TO MEET GOD'S NEEDS
-- is to meet the needs of one of His children.

God's Supernatural Power

Matt 25:34-40 **Final test at the judgment**
For I was an hungred, and ye gave me meat: I was thirsty,
.. a stranger, .. naked, .. sick, .. prison, and ye came unto me.
....Inasmuch as ye have done it unto one of the least of
these my brethren, ye have done it unto me.

The Born-again Christian's dual nature

Son of Man	Son of God
Body & Soul	**Spirit**
- Man's Ability	- God's Ability
(What man can do -- good deeds)	(Anointing -- what God can do through man)

1. Natural   **2.** Supernatural

Man's needs:	Man's needs:
- Hungry	- Hungry
- Thirsty	- Thirsty
- Sick	- Sick
- Stranger (lonely)	- Stranger (lonely)
- Prison	- Prison

(1) Building a relationship with someone in need by doing kind deeds, as a **son of man**. These good deeds (what we can do) begin to open up the channel of God's love and compassion in our lives for the second step.

(2) God's supernatural power -- what God can do through us, as a **son of God**, to minister to their needs.

Chart R-7

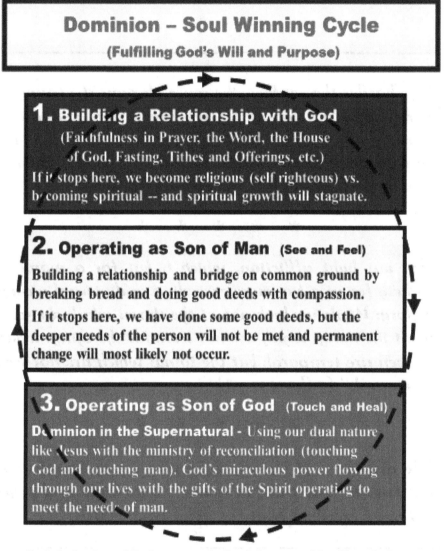

Dominion – Soul Winning Cycle
(Fulfilling God's Will and Purpose)

1. Building a Relationship with God
(Faithfulness in Prayer, the Word, the House of God, Fasting, Tithes and Offerings, etc.)
If it stops here, we become religious (self righteous) vs. becoming spiritual -- and spiritual growth will stagnate.

2. Operating as Son of Man (See and Feel)
Building a relationship and bridge on common ground by breaking bread and doing good deeds with compassion.
If it stops here, we have done some good deeds, but the deeper needs of the person will not be met and permanent change will most likely not occur.

3. Operating as Son of God (Touch and Heal)
Dominion in the Supernatural - Using our dual nature like Jesus with the ministry of reconciliation (touching God and touching man). God's miraculous power flowing through our lives with the gifts of the Spirit operating to meet the needs of man.

Soul winning is a spiritual process and will only be successful and have lasting results as we operate in the Spirit. To operate at this level the first two processes are foundational and cannot be bypassed. You cannot have compassion on someone that you cannot see and touch. As we complete this cycle over and over again, true and lasting spiritual growth of the born-again Christian occurs.

"The harder the conflict, the more glorious the triumph. What we obtain too cheap, we esteem too lightly; it is dearness only that gives everything its value. I love the man that can smile in trouble, that can gather strength from distress and grow." (Thomas Paine)

*　*　*　*　*

"For our light affliction, which is but for a moment, worketh for us a far more exceeding and eternal weight of glory; While we look not at the things which are seen, but at the things which are not seen: for the things which are seen are temporal; but the things which are not seen are eternal." (2 Cor 4:17, 18)

*　*　*　*　*

"He cleanses and repeatedly prunes every branch that continues to bear fruit, to make it bear more and richer and more excellent fruit." (John 15:2) AMP

3. When the Answer to Prayer is "No" or "Wait"

3.1 The Implication of God's Foreknowledge

Before addressing the subject of "denied" or "delayed" answers to prayer, we will briefly discuss two related foundational principles regarding the implication of God's goodness and foreknowledge:

(a) All things work together for the good of a Christian.

(b) God intervenes in our lives because of His foreknowledge of our future.

(a) God's promise that all things, "good" or "bad" work for our good.

Apostle Paul records one of the greatest promises and hopes for a child of God in his letter to the Romans: *"And we know that **all things** work together for good to them that love God, to them who are the called according to his purpose."*

This is a great guarantee -- **all things, good or bad work for**

our good. But it is very important to understand what he does not say. He does not guarantee that everything that comes into our lives will be good. Apostle Paul understood this well because he suffered a lot of persecution and opposition in his life for God:

"Of the Jews five times received I forty stripes save one. Thrice was I beaten with rods, once was I stoned, thrice I suffered shipwreck, a night and a day I have been in the deep; In journeyings often, in perils of waters, in perils of robbers, in perils by mine own countrymen, in perils by the heathen, in perils in the city, in perils in the wilderness, in perils in the sea, in perils among false brethren; In weariness and painfulness, in watchings often, in hunger and thirst, in fastings often, in cold and nakedness" (2 Cor. 11:24-27).

Apostle Paul's response to all his suffering was that all of this happened to him for the advancement of God's Kingdom and his salvation: *"But I would that ye understand, brethren, that **the things which happened unto me have been for the furtherance of the gospel.** For I know that this shall turn to my salvation through your prayer, and the supply of the Spirit of Jesus Christ" (Phil. 1:12, 19).*

Paul says if we give our lives to God, we have a benefit that people in the world don't have. They go through the same trouble and difficulties that we go through. But the difference between the Christian and the unbeliever is not that one suffers trouble and the other doesn't. The Christian has God's assurance that He will take everything in our life, the good things, the bad things, the happy things, the sad things and work them all together for our good. Ultimately, we will be rewarded the gift of eternal life in the world to come. Nobody in the world but a child of God has that promise.

(b) God intervenes in our lives because of His foreknowledge of our future.

Apostle Paul goes on to state in the next verse, *Rom. 8:29:* *"For whom he did **foreknow**, he also did **predestinate to be conformed to the image of his Son**, that he might be the firstborn among many brethren."* Here we have two important concepts, predestination and foreknowledge which are summarized below.

Predestination

God has predestinated the church for glory and eternal life in heaven. God does not predestinate individuals; our assurance of heaven is conditional. A few of the many Scriptures that declare this truth are listed here.

2 Cor. 6:17
*Wherefore **come out** from among them, and **be ye separate**, saith the Lord, and **touch not the unclean thing; and I will receive you,***

2 Peter 1:5-7, 10, 21
*And beside this, giving all diligence, add to your faith virtue; and to virtue knowledge . . . temperance . . . patience . . . godliness . . . brotherly kindness . . . charity. Wherefore the rather, brethren, give diligence to make your calling and election sure: **for if ye do these things, ye shall never fall:***

*21 Not every one that saith unto me, Lord, Lord, shall enter into the kingdom of heaven; but **he that doeth the will of my Father which is in heaven.***

Rev. 3:5
He that overcometh**, the same shall be clothed in white raiment; and **I will not blot out his name out of the book of life.

155

God does not predestinate individuals, but He has predestinated His church for glory in eternity. Keep yourself in the church, because nothing can destroy the church of the living God. Jesus states in *Matthew 16:18: "Upon this rock I will build my church; and the gates of hell shall not prevail against it."*

Neither the devil, nor hell, nor any opposition on earth can prevail against the child of God that remains in the church of Jesus Christ: *"For I am persuaded, that neither death, nor life, nor angels, nor principalities, nor powers, nor things present, nor things to come, Nor height, nor depth, nor any other creature, shall be able to separate us from the love of God, which is in Christ Jesus our Lord" (Rom. 8:38, 39).*

Foreknowledge Vs. Predestination

God in His supernatural foreknowledge sees the end from the beginning: *"I am God, and there is none else; I am God, and there is none like me, declaring the end from the beginning, and from ancient times the things that are not yet done" (Isa. 46:9, 10). "Time and again I told you what was going to happen in the future" (Isa. 48:3). TLB*

To better understand foreknowledge, as it pertains to our personal lives, let's look at a practical example. In this setting, someone is in an elevated position, in a high tower, and observes two cars approaching on a blind curve. All of a sudden one of the cars crosses the line into the path of the approaching vehicle. The person in the elevated position has foreknowledge of the auto crash, but has nothing to do with the resulting disaster.

Another example would be the person in the tower watching a car approaching a bridge that has been washed out. The person in the elevated position has foreknowledge of the car plunging off the bank of a washed out bridge, but has nothing to do with the resulting disaster.

However, if a person with foreknowledge, because of their elevated position, had a way to intervene or communicate with the drivers of these cars, the two disasters could have been avoided. Likewise, our great omnipotent, omniscient God who sits high above the earth, observes every detail of our lives in the future. And in His love and mercy He intervenes to alter the direction and path of our life.

Isa. 40:22
He sits enthroned above the circle of the earth, and its people are like grasshoppers.

Isa. 66:1
Thus saith the Lord, the heaven is my throne, and the earth is my footstool.

2 Chron. 16:9
For the eyes of the Lord run to and fro throughout the whole earth, to shew himself strong in the behalf of them whose heart is perfect toward him.

God, in His supernatural foreknowledge, sees when our lives will get off course in the future. In His mercy, He sends or allows situations (troubles and trials) to alter our course and get us back on the highway to heaven. God's ultimate purpose and will for our lives is for us to be saved and to be: *"Conformed to the image of His son."* God wants us to become more like Him -- to be a partaker of His divine nature.

157

The Vital Importance of Prayer

Rick Warren states in his book, *The Purpose Driven Life:* "Life is a series of problems: Either you are in one now, you're just coming out of one, or you're getting ready to go into another one. The reason for this is that: **God is more interested in your character than your comfort. God is more interested in making your life holy than He is in making your life happy.** We can be reasonably happy here on earth, but that's not the goal of life. The goal is to grow in character, in Christ likeness."

God uses events in our lives to make us into His image. Someone once said: "When Jesus came into my heart, I thought He would hang a few pictures and make a few minor changes. But He came in and started remodeling -- tearing down walls and making major changes." These changes most often are manifest as troubles and trials.

We encounter these difficulties and trials for different reasons and we are not always told why. Jonah was in a storm because he was out of God's will. The apostle Paul was in a storm because other people on the boat were out of God's will. The disciples experienced a storm while in the will of God. Jesus was the One who told them, let's go to the other side. Then before they arrived, they experienced a great storm.

So there are unlimited reasons and ways that we face storms in life. And we may never understand exactly why. But there is one thing we know from God's Word. And that is, "If we love God and pursue His purpose, He will take all things and work them together for our good."

3.2 Why Prayers May be Denied of Delayed

It is indisputable from the numerous Scriptures in the Old and New Testaments that God has provided healing and deliverance from trouble, trial and affliction. But the very provision for healing confirms there will be sickness that requires healing. The provision for deliverance alerts us to the troubles and trials that will require it. The assurance of the awesome peace of God signifies there will be storms:

- Battle precedes victory,
  - Sickness precedes healing,
    - Trouble precedes deliverance.

An understanding of this principle will protect our faith and give us hope and patience to wait for God's will and timing for the healing and deliverance for which we sincerely pray.

There are times when prayers are immediately and miraculously granted. But the provision of healing and deliverance, invoked in sincere and urgent prayer, does not ensure immediate deliverance. Our trust in God is tested in trouble and trial. Delays in answer to our prayers develop patience and maturity. This is a challenging subject to address because it is often difficult for us to embrace the concept that it is God's plan for us to suffer awhile: *"After you have suffered a little while . . . our God will give you his eternal glory."*

There is a time of trusting God, searching our hearts and humbling ourselves, while we wait for God's work in our lives to be accomplished. Our attitude should mirror that of Job: **"Although he slay me, yet will I trust in him. And when He has tried me I shall come forth as pure gold."**

159

The Vital Importance of Prayer

To understand affliction, we must rise above the temporal:

- To heights with God and see from His perspective.
- Looking beyond our natural life to eternal life.

The writings of apostle Paul in the New Testament and Habakkuk from the Old Testament reflect this concept.

Apostle Paul is in a Roman prison and will be beheaded and not delivered. He is not focusing on the terrible circumstances but on eternal life -- and he writes: *"Rejoice in the Lord always."*

Phil. 4:4, 6, 7
*4 **Rejoice in the Lord always**: and again I say, Rejoice.*
6 Be careful for nothing; but in everything by prayer and supplication with thanksgiving let your requests be made known unto God.
7 And the peace of God, which passeth all understanding, shall keep your hearts and minds through Christ Jesus.

Habakkuk records a bankrupt situation where everything was lost. His testimony during this time of great loss is: *"Rejoice in the Lord."*

Hab. 3:17-19
17 Although the fig tree shall not blossom, neither shall fruit be in the vines; the labour of the olive shall fail, and the fields shall yield no meat; the flock shall be cut off from the fold, and there shall be no herd in the stalls:
*18 **Yet I will rejoice in the Lord, I will joy in the God of my salvation.***
19 The Lord God is my strength, and he will make my feet like hinds' feet, and he will make me to walk upon mine high places.

160

In this chapter we examine God's Word to better understand when some prayers are answered and others are delayed or denied. When things do not work out the way we have prayed, we can confidently know that He has a purpose and plan for our benefit which are beyond our understanding.

- **Sometimes God chooses to change us rather than change our situation.**

God is sovereign. He has all authority, power, and dominion. He is without limitation and does all things well. God has all wisdom and knows the future. He knows what is best for us and has never made a mistake with one life. His ways and thoughts are higher than ours: *"For as the heavens are higher than the earth, so are my ways higher than your ways, and my thoughts than your thoughts"* (Isa. 55:9).

Isa. 40:13, 14, 22, 25-28
13 Who can advise the Spirit of the Lord or be his teacher or give him counsel?
14 Has he ever needed anyone's advice? Did he need instruction as to what is right and best?
22 It is God who sits above the circle of the earth. (The people below must seem to him like grasshoppers!) He is the one who stretches out the heavens like a curtain and makes his tent from them.
25 "With whom will you compare me? Who is my equal?" asks the Holy One.
26 Look up into the heavens! Who created all these stars? As a shepherd leads his sheep, calling each by its pet name, and counts them to see that none are lost or strayed, so God does with stars and planets!
*27 O Jacob, O Israel, **how can you say that the Lord doesn't***

see your troubles and isn't being fair?
28 Don't you yet understand? Don't you know by now that the everlasting God, the Creator of the farthest parts of the earth, never grows faint or weary? No one can fathom the depths of his understanding. TLB

- **Sometimes one's faith in God is damaged when they are told that if they had enough faith, God would heal them or change their situation -- but the answer did not come.**

Healing and deliverance are specific promises in God's Word, but He is sovereign; His purpose and timing is superior to ours. We are just called to serve and trust Him, submitting to the process of fiery trial.

If our love for God is pure, we can unconditionally trust Him, making no demands for deliverance. When we love and trust God, we will be willing to pray: "God, I really want this need met, but I want Your will more -- Thy will be done." This attitude of trust removes fear and releases faith, enabling God to work on our behalf.

- **We must give God permission to do whatever it takes (trial or deliverance) to bring us to eternal life.**

3.2.1 No Human Reasoning for Unanswered Prayers

Jesus predicts the future suffering of James: *"And he saith unto them, ye shall drink indeed of my cup, and be baptized with the baptism that I am baptized with: but to sit on my right hand, and on my left, is not mine to give, but it shall be given to them for whom it is prepared of my Father" (Matt. 20:23).*

Jesus predicts the long life of Peter: *"Verily, verily, I say unto thee, when thou wast young, thou girdedst thyself, and walkedst whither thou wouldest: but* **when thou shalt be old,** *thou shalt stretch forth thy hands, and another shall gird thee, and carry thee whither thou wouldest not" (John 21:18).*

When Peter asks about what will happen to John, Jesus replies that was none of his concern: *"Jesus saith unto him, if I will that he tarry till I come,* **what is that to thee**? *Follow thou me" (John 21:22).*

James was imprisoned by King Herod and then executed with the sword. Herod then arrested Peter with the same intention to be carried out after the Passover. However, the church prayed fervently for Peter and God sent an angel for a miraculous deliverance. James did not receive his deliverance, but it was not attributed to a lack of faith or the church's failure to pray. There is no human reasoning to explain deliverance for one and death for other; all we know is that it was within the plan of God.

John the Baptist, the forerunner of Jesus Christ, after a great ministry, was imprisoned and executed by King Herod. He was referred to by Jesus as "great". But when Jesus' ministry began, instead of being selected as one of the disciples, he was beheaded in prison. God's plan for John brought death, not the deliverance for which he and others had undoubtedly sincerely prayed.

Matt. 11:2-5, 11
2 Now when John had heard in the prison the works of Christ, he sent two of his disciples,
3 And said unto him, art thou he that should come, or do we look for another?
4 Jesus answered and said unto them, go and shew John again those things which ye do hear and see:
5 The blind receive their sight, and the lame walk, the lepers are cleansed, and the deaf hear, the dead are raised up, and the poor have the Gospel preached to them.
11 Verily I say unto you, Among them that are born of women there hath not risen a greater than John the Baptist: notwithstanding he that is least in the kingdom of heaven is greater than he.

In this setting, Jesus spoke a truth that we must accept when our prayers for deliverance are not in God's will and are denied: ***"Blessed is he, whosoever shall not be offended in me"*** *(Matt. 11:6).*

-- From "The Pulpit Commentary"
Verse 6 - And blessed is he, whosoever shall not be offended in me: shall find none occasion of stumbling in me, but exhibits perfect trust under delay and disappointment.[1]

3.2.2 Trial and Testing Develops Christian Character
When God wants to educate us, He does not enroll us in the school of graces, but in the school of testing. The fire of God's furnace is used to identify and remove the impurities that would hinder God's eternal purpose and will for our lives.

The prophet Zechariah states: *"I will bring the third part through the fire, and will refine them as silver is refined, and will try them as gold is tried: they shall call on my name, and I will hear them: I will say, It is my people: and they shall say, The LORD is my God" (Zech. 13:9).*

-- From "Barnes' Notes"

As gold that is tried in the crucible, and that comes forth the more pure, the more intense is the heat. The application of fire to it serves to separate every particle of impurity or alloy, and leaves only the pure metal. So it is with trials applied to the child of God.

A true Christian should not dread trial. It will not hurt him. He will be the more valuable for his trials, as gold is for the application of heat. There is no danger of destroying his faith. It will live in the flames, and will survive the raging heat.[2]

Great leaders emerge when crises occurs. In the lives of achievers, we read terrible circumstances which forced them above the commonplace. Not only did they find the answer, but discovered a tremendous power within themselves. As Christians, we discover God's tremendous power as we submit to trial and suffering.

In the athletic, business, and spiritual worlds, it is impossible to succeed without suffering. When Glen Cunningham was eight years old, his doctor told him he would never walk again after suffering severe leg burns from a gasoline explosion. Through grueling discipline and rehabilitation, he became one of the premiere milers, starring in the 1932 Olympics.

"If you are successful and have not suffered, probably someone preceding you has suffered. If you are suffering without success, perhaps someone after you may succeed. But there is no success and significant improvement without self-denial and trial."[3]

There are no easy steps to maturity or secrets of instant sainthood. When God wants to make a giant oak, He takes a hundred years, but when he wants to make a mushroom, He does it overnight. Great souls are grown through struggles and storms and seasons of suffering. The apostle James tells us to be patient with the process: *"Don't try to get out of anything prematurely. Let it do its work so you become mature and well-developed" (James 1:4). MSG*

When Habakkuk became depressed because he didn't think God was acting quickly enough, God had this to say: *"These things I plan won't happen right away. Slowly, steadily, surely, the time approaches when the vision will be fulfilled. If it seems slow, do not despair, for these things will surely come to pass. Just be patient! They will not be overdue a single day!" (Habakkuk 2:3). TLB*

We must trust God even when we don't understand; confident He is working on our eternal life. We are often blind to the eternal purpose of God, looking only at the temporal. The Refiner's fire and the way of the cross is often God's plan to bring change to our lives.

- **Misunderstanding of this concept sometimes causes Christians to become discouraged or lose faith when they don't understand God's process and their prayer for deliverance is delayed or even denied.**

Acts 14:22
*Confirming the souls of the disciples, and exhorting them to continue in the faith, and that we must through **much***

tribulation enter *into the kingdom of God.*

Tribulation is a part of God's plan that includes difficult circumstances and sometimes affliction that brings pain, distress or grief. This may be a testing process, not because of sin, but to develop character and propel us into the next phase of God's purpose for our lives.

Just as fire is used in the process to strengthen steel, the Bible is filled with examples of how God uses the fires of tribulation to develop character, especially in leaders. Some of the characters in the Bible that experienced the fires of tribulation include:

Moses: God took eighty years to develop Moses, including forty years in the wilderness, to prepare him to lead Israel from Egyptian bondage. He was demoted from the comforts of Pharaoh's palace to the status of a lowly shepherd for 40 years. For 14,600 days Moses kept waiting while tending his father-in-law's sheep on the back side of the desert. During this time, God was preparing him to lead His people through a hot burning desert. Also, God was changing Moses on the inside, from the overconfident prince in Pharaoh's palace, to the meek and humble servant that He could trust. One day he was a poor, lowly shepherd and the next day he commanded a nation of two million people. In our desert moments, we must not get fixated on getting out of the desert and forget that God is at work in our life.

Joseph endured the pit and the dungeon before being promoted to the throne of the most powerful nation in the world. When the sun rose one morning, he was a prisoner in a foreign land with no hope of escape; accused of a crime punishable by death. But before the sun set that day, he was wearing the Egyptian king's royal robe, second in command to the ruler of the most powerful nation in the world.

David was threatened and had to flee for his life during the years between his anointing and ruling on the throne. After years of testing, he received a great promotion to be king of Judah and later over all the tribes of Israel.

The three Hebrew children endured the fire before they were promoted in Babylon. After the fiery furnace their God was recognized and exalted by King Nebuchadnezzar and an entire nation.

Job experienced terrible heartbreak and loss in the will of God. He stated, during the painful process of losing his possessions, children and health: *"Behold, I go forward, but he is not there; and backward, but I cannot perceive him: On the left hand, where he doth work, but I cannot behold him: he hideth himself on the right hand, that I cannot see him: 10 But he knoweth the way that I take: when he hath tried me, I shall come forth as gold."* He was saying: "God, I don't know where You are, but You know where I am. And when my trial has ended, I shall emerge as pure gold."

At the end of his trial Job was restored and received twice what he owned before his loss and acknowledged that God allows trials in our life for our good: *"Behold, happy is the man whom **God correcteth**: therefore despise not thou the chastening of the Almighty: For **he maketh sore**, and bindeth up: **he woundeth**, and his hands make whole. He shall deliver thee in **six troubles**: yea, in seven there shall no evil touch thee. In **famine** he shall redeem thee from death: and in **war** from the power of the sword" (Job 5:17-20).*

Apostle James states: *"Blessed is the man that endureth* ***temptation:*** **(adversity, discipline)** *for when he is tried, he shall receive the crown of life, which the Lord hath promised to them that love him" (James 1:12).*

Apostle Peter states that our short term suffering will produce eternal results: *"And **after you have suffered a little while**, the God of all grace [Who imparts all blessing and favor], Who has called you to His [own] eternal glory in Christ Jesus, will Himself complete and make you what you ought to be, establish and ground you securely, and strengthen, and settle you" (1 Peter 5:10). AMP*

Apostle Paul tells us that in the future we will become, but until then we must overcome: *"Moreover [let us also be full of joy now!] let us exult and triumph in our troubles and rejoice in our sufferings, knowing that **pressure and affliction and hardship produce patient and unswerving endurance. And endurance (fortitude) develops maturity of character** (approved faith and tried integrity). And character [of this sort] produces [the habit of] joyful and confident hope of eternal salvation" (Rom. 5:3, 4). AMP*

Apostle Paul also states that God corrects and chastens us for our good: *"And ye have forgotten the exhortation which speaketh unto you as unto children, my son, despise not thou the chastening of the Lord, nor faint when thou art rebuked of him: **For whom the Lord loveth he chasteneth, and scourgeth every son whom he receiveth.** If ye endure chastening, God dealeth with you as with sons; for what son is he whom the father chasteneth not? But if ye be without chastisement, whereof all are partakers, then are ye bastards, and not sons. Furthermore we have had fathers of our flesh which corrected us, and we gave them reverence: shall we not much rather be* *in subjection unto the father of spirits, and live? For they verily for a few days chastened us after their own pleasure; but he **for our profit, that we might be partakers of his holiness.** Now no chastening for the present seemeth to be joyous, but grievous: nevertheless afterward it yieldeth the peaceable **fruit of righteousness** unto them which are exercised thereby" (Heb. 12:5-11).*

Jesus, in the Sermon on the Mount, teaches that He will prune our lives to make us bear more fruit: *"Any branch in Me that does not bear fruit [that stops bearing] He cuts away (trims off, takes away); and He cleanses and repeatedly prunes every branch that continues to bear fruit, to make it bear more and richer and more excellent fruit. I am the Vine; you are the branches. Whoever lives in Me and I in him bears much (abundant) fruit. However, apart from Me [cut off from vital union with Me] you can do nothing" (John 15:2, 5). AMP*

King David observes that the right response for affliction is a broken heart and a contrite spirit: *"The righteous cry, and the Lord heareth, and delivereth them out of all their troubles. The Lord is nigh unto them that are of a broken heart; And saveth such as be of a contrite spirit" (Psalms 34:17, 18).*

3.2.3 Faith and Deliverance Vs. Faith without Deliverance

The key to receiving deliverance and surviving when deliverance is not experienced, is our faith and trust in God. Hebrews, Chapter 11 is the faith chapter. However, there are two distinct parts to the chapter:

- In the **first part**, they experienced victory and deliverance.
- In the **second part**, they did not receive deliverance, however, they obtained a good report through faith.

More faith is required in our Christian walk when we do not receive the answer to our prayer for deliverance.

Heb. 11:1-35 (Part 1 - Received Their Deliverance)

1 Now faith is the substance of things hoped for, the evidence of things not seen. 2 For by it the elders obtained a good report. 3 Through faith we understand that the worlds were framed by the word of God, so that things which are seen were not made of things which do appear. 4-32 By faith Abel . . . By faith Enoch . . . By faith Noah . . . By faith Abraham . . . By faith Sara . . . By faith Isaac . . . By faith Jacob . . . By faith Joseph . . . By faith Moses . . . By faith the harlot Rahab . . .Gideon . . . Barak . . . Samson . . . David . . . 33 Who through faith subdued kingdoms, wrought righteousness, obtained promises, stopped the mouths of lions 34 Quenched the violence of fire, escaped the edge of the sword, out of weakness were made strong, waxed valiant in fight, turned to flight the armies of the aliens. 35 Women received their dead raised to life again.

Heb. 11:35-39 (Part 2 - Did Not Receive Their Deliverance)

35 And others were tortured, not accepting deliverance; that they might obtain a better resurrection: 36 And others had trial of cruel mockings and scourgings, yea, moreover of bonds and imprisonment: 37 They were stoned, they were sawn asunder, were tempted, were slain with the sword: they wandered about in sheepskins and goatskins; being destitute, afflicted, tormented; 38 (Of whom the world was not worthy:) they wandered in deserts, and in mountains, and in dens and caves of the earth. 39 And these all, having obtained a good report through faith, received not the promise.

They all had faith, but God's plan was for promotion to eternal

171

life. While the Bible gives a general promise of healing to the church, it may not be the will of God to heal instantly in a specific case. Our prayers and our will must be subject to the will of God. Jesus instructs us to pray: *"Thy kingdom come.* ***Thy will be done*** *in earth, as it is in heaven."*

The answer to prayer for sickness or trouble may be:

- **Instant**, Paul and Silas were miraculously delivered within twelve hours of their imprisonment.
- **Answered**, with a gradual process of healing.
- **Denied**, dying in the faith and receiving the answer in the resurrection. The disciples and many other Christians died as martyrs.
- **Denied**, God's grace will provide strength to endure, like apostle Paul's request for God to remove the thorn in his flesh:

2 Cor. 12:7-10
7 And lest I should be exalted above measure through the abundance of the revelations, there was given to me a thorn in the flesh, the messenger of Satan to buffet me, lest I should be exalted above measure.
8 For this thing I besought the Lord thrice, that it might depart from me.
9 And he said unto me, My grace is sufficient for thee: for my strength is made perfect in weakness. Most gladly therefore will I rather glory in my infirmities, that the power of Christ may rest upon me.
10 Therefore I take pleasure in infirmities, in reproaches, in necessities, in persecutions, in distresses for Christ's sake: for when I am weak, then am I strong.

3.2.4 Twelve Apostles' Final Testimony Written in Blood

Doubtless, these great men and the churches of their day prayed for deliverance and protection. But they embraced the will of God and their final testimonies were written in blood.

	Apostle	Summary	Death
1	Andrew	- Introduced Peter to Jesus. - Brought the lad with 5 loaves and fishes to Jesus. - Brother of Peter.	**Martyr** - Crucified at Patrae, Achaia (southern Greece). Hung alive on the cross two days, exhorting spectators.
2	Bartholomew	- Jesus saw him under a fig tree.	**Martyr** - Crucified by the idolaters of India. Preached the gospel in Mesopotamia (Iraq), Persia (Iran) and India.
3	James	- A fisherman. - With Jesus in Gethsemane.	**Martyr** - Killed 10 years after the first martyr, Stephen. His accuser was converted by James' courage and both were beheaded.
4	James	- Called James, the less, (younger). - First Bishop of Jerusalem.	**Martyr** – At age 90, stoned by Jews.
5	John	- Known as the "beloved disciple". - At foot of cross with Jesus' mother. - Brother of James.	**Natural Death** - The only apostle who did not die a martyr's death. Banished by Roman Emperor Domitian to Isle of Patmos where he received the Revelation of Jesus Christ.

Twelve Apostles' Final Testimony Written in Blood

	Apostle	Summary	Death
6	Judas Iscariot	- Treasurer of the apostolic group. - He betrayed Jesus for 30 pieces of silver.	**Suicide** - Judas cast down the 30 pieces of silver in the temple, and went out and hung himself.
	Matthias	Took Judas' place.	**Martyr** - Stoned at Jerusalem.
7	Jude	- Writer, Book of Jude.	**Martyr** - Crucified 72 AD at city of Edessa (Turkey).
8	Matthew	- Also called Levi. - Tax collector for the Romans.	**Martyr** - Killed with a sword about 60AD.
9	Peter	- A fisherman whom Jesus called the Rock. - First Bishop of Rome.	**Martyr** - Crucified at Rome under Nero. Crucified up-side-down; did not consider himself worthy to be crucified like Jesus.
10	Phillip	- Brought Bartholomew (Nathaniel) to Jesus.	**Martyr** - Crucified about 54AD. Preached the gospel in Phrygia, the Roman Province of Asia near Ephesus (Turkey).
11	Simon	- Called "The Zealot" because he was associated with that sect.	**Martyr** - Crucified in Britain in 74AD. Also preached in Africa.
12	Thomas	- A fisherman on the same crew as Peter and Andrew. - Called the "doubter".	**Martyr** - Killed with a spear in India. Preached the gospel in Parthia (Iran) and in Kerala (southern India).

In addition to the twelve apostles the following were also martyrs:

- Mark was dragged to death.
- Luke was hanged on an olive tree.
- Paul was beheaded by the Emperor Nero at Rome.

- **If we are willing to give our lives for the gospel's sake, we will embrace the cross and more easily accept fiery trial as God's will.**

3.2.5 Revelation of God to Unbelievers Through Miracles

Jesus ministered healing and deliverance to the needs of individuals because of His great compassion. He first addressed their physical needs, to **reveal Himself to them;** He then ministered to their spiritual needs.

The miracles of Jesus:
- Attracted the attention of the multitudes.
- Facilitated reaching the most people in the least amount of time (much to do in the short time of His ministry).
- Caused people to abandon traditions held for many generations.
- Confirmed His teachings.
- Affirmed He was the Messiah.

Jesus' prayer at the tomb of Lazarus indicates this revelatory purpose: *"That they may believe that thou hast sent me."*

John 11:41-45
41 Then they took away the stone from the place where the dead was laid. And Jesus lifted up his eyes, and said, Father, I thank thee that thou hast heard me.
*42 And I knew that thou hearest me always: **but because of***

the people which stand by I said it, that they may believe that thou hast sent me.

43 And when he thus had spoken, he cried with a loud voice, Lazarus, come forth.

44 And he that was dead came forth, bound hand and foot with grave clothes: and his face was bound about with a napkin Jesus saith unto them, Loose him, and let him go.

*45 Then many of the Jews which came to Mary, and had **seen** the things which Jesus did, believed on him.*

The following are a few of the many Scriptures concerning Jesus' healing ministry. Many times He healed them all, **revealing His identity as the Messiah.**

Matt. 4:24
*And his fame went throughout all Syria: and they brought unto him **all sick people** that were taken with divers diseases and torments, and those which were possessed with devils, and those which were lunatick, and those that had the palsy; and **he healed them**.*

Mark 3:10, 11
*10 For he had **healed many**; insomuch that they pressed upon him for to touch him, as many as had plagues.*
*11 And unclean spirits, when they saw him, fell down before him, and cried, saying, **Thou art the Son of God**.*

Luke 4:40
*Now when the sun was setting, all they that had any sick with divers diseases brought them unto him; and **he laid his hands on every one of them, and healed them**.*

Matt. 15:31
Insomuch that the multitude wondered, *when they saw the dumb to speak, the maimed to be whole, the lame to walk, and*

the blind to see: and **they glorified the God of Israel.**

Mark 6:2
*And when the sabbath day was come, he began to teach in the synagogue: and many hearing him were astonished, saying, From whence hath this man these things? and what wisdom is this which is given unto him, that even such **mighty works are wrought by his hands**?*

Mark 7:37
*And were beyond measure astonished, saying, **He hath done all things well**: he maketh both the deaf to hear, and the dumb to speak.*

Luke 7:16
*And there came a fear on all: and they glorified God, saying, That a great prophet is risen up among us; and, That **God hath visited his people.***

John 9:33
If this man were not of God, he could do nothing.

Matt. 8:16
*When the even was come, they brought unto him many that were possessed with devils: and he cast out the spirits with his word, and **healed all that were sick**:*

We must not expect that because Jesus healed everyone in some Scripture settings during His ministry, that it is His will to heal everyone, every time. Scripture states that it may be the will of God for us, as Christians, to endure adversity for a season of testing. Apostle Peter experienced and taught the concept that we must embrace the cross (suffering and trial) and even rejoice that God is working to change us.

1 Peter 4:12, 13, 19
12 Dear friends, don't be surprised at the fiery trials you are
going through, as if something strange were happening to you.
13 Instead, be very glad -- for these trials make you partners
with Christ in his suffering, so that you will have the wonderful
joy of seeing his glory when it is revealed to all the world.
19 So if you are suffering in a manner that pleases God, keep
on doing what is right, and trust your lives to the God who
created you, for he will never fail you. NLT

The goodness of God leads men to repentance. If a sinner
is honestly seeking to know God, He will often reveal Himself
to them through a miracle: *"God's kindness is intended to lead*
you to repent [to change your mind and inner man to accept
God's will]" (Rom. 2:4) AMP. This concept should elevate
our faith, thrusting us further into the harvest field to reach
sinners, like Jesus, with a ministry of miracles and salvation.

- **The true love of God, flowing through our lives as
  Christians, should allow us to be more concerned about
  the sinner's need of a miracle than our own (loving our
  neighbor as ourselves). This attitude is imperative if we
  are to become a harvest-driven vs. a maintenance-
  driven Christian.**

- **Although we may be suffering an affliction, we can still
  pray the prayer of faith for a sinner having the same
  affliction.**

- **Sometimes when we connect with God and unselfishly
  pray the prayer of faith for someone else, the healing
  virtue that flows to heal them will also heal us.**

178

3.2.6 Answers Delayed Because of Sin

Sometimes we have a narrow definition of sin and become self-righteous when we live above the sins of the flesh. However, there are many types of sin:

- Sins of the flesh (works of the flesh).
- Sins of the soul (my will, mind and emotions conflicting with God's will, mind and agape love).
- Sins of the spirit (resisting the Spirit, or overriding the conscience).

Any kind of disobedience is sin. Obedience is not only saying, "no" to the devil, but saying, "yes" to God's will. Failing to do God's will is disobedience, which is sin. Sometimes trial and affliction is the only thing that will bring our will into alignment with His will.

Psalms 66:18
If I regard iniquity in my heart, the Lord will not hear me:

Psalms 119:67, 68, 71
67 Before I was afflicted I went astray: but now have I kept thy word.
68 Thou art good, and doest good; teach me thy statutes.
71 It is good for me that I have been afflicted; that I might learn thy statutes.

Psalms 25:17, 18
17 The troubles of my heart are enlarged: O bring thou me out of my distresses.
18 Look upon mine affliction and my pain; and forgive all my sins.

Psalms 119:135, 136, 153
135 Make thy face to shine upon thy servant; and teach me thy

statutes.

136 Rivers of waters run down mine eyes, because they keep not thy law.

153 Consider mine affliction, and deliver me: for I do not forget thy law.

We can't approach God unless our hands are clean. This means our hearts are clean and our relationships with others are clean: *"Lord, who shall abide in thy tabernacle? who shall dwell in thy holy hill? He that walketh uprightly, and worketh righteousness, and speaketh the truth in his heart. He that backbiteth not with his tongue, nor doeth evil to his neighbour, nor taketh up a reproach against his neighbour"* (Psalms 15:1-3). *"Who shall ascend into the hill of the Lord? or who shall stand in his holy place? He that hath clean hands, and a pure heart; who hath not lifted up his soul unto vanity, nor sworn deceitfully"* (Psalms 24:3, 4).

The apostle James connects repentance to the promise for healing: *"And the prayer of faith shall save the sick, and the Lord shall raise him up; and if he have committed sins, they shall be forgiven him. Confess your faults one to another, and pray one for another, that ye may be healed. The effectual fervent prayer of a righteous man availeth much"* (James 5:15, 16).

Rev. 3:19
As many as I love, I rebuke and chasten: be zealous therefore, and repent.

3.2.7 Trials Become Testimonies to Others

Victories over difficulties become our greatest testimonies and are examples of strength to others. How can we testify of the healing, delivering, and keeping power of God until we have experienced tribulations?

- **There will be no testimony without a test.**

2 Cor. 1:4-7
*4 He comforts us in all our troubles **so that we can comfort others**. When others are troubled, we will be able to **give them the same comfort God has given us**.*
5 You can be sure that the more we suffer for Christ, the more God will shower us with his comfort through Christ.
6 So when we are weighed down with troubles, it is for your benefit and salvation! For when God comforts us, it is so that we, in turn, can be an encouragement to you. Then you can patiently endure the same things we suffer.
7 We are confident that as you share in suffering, you will also share God's comfort. NLT

3.2.8 Sickness Unto Death -- Promotion to a Better World

There is a sickness unto death, thus no healing or deliverance -- until it is received in eternal life. Jesus cited this when Lazarus died, *"This sickness is not unto death"*-- because Lazarus would soon live again when Jesus summoned him out of the tomb.

John 11:4
*When Jesus heard that, he said, **this sickness is not unto death**, but for the glory of God, that the son of God might be glorified thereby.*

Elderly Saints - There is a sickness unto death when elderly people, who have lived a full life, are called home: *"The days of our years are threescore years and ten; and if by reason of strength they be fourscore years, yet is their strength labour and sorrow; for it is soon cut off, and we fly away"* *(Psalms 90:10)*.

Death for Salvation - In some terminally ill situations, God has possibly taken some home, perhaps because they failed to live for Him when in good health. God alone can see the future.

Untimely Death - A sickness unto death results for those who have completed their work on earth and God promotes them to a better place, where there is no sickness and no crying. In our world untimely death refers to age; but God sees from a different perspective.

Psalms 116:15
Precious in the sight of the Lord is the death of his saints.

1 Cor. 15:54, 55
54 So when this corruptible shall have put on incorruption, and this mortal shall have put on immortality, then shall be brought to pass the saying that is written, Death is swallowed up in victory.
55 O death, where is thy sting? O grave, where is thy victory?

Rev. 21:4
And God shall wipe away all tears from their eyes; and there shall be no more death, neither sorrow, nor crying, neither shall there be any more pain: for the former things are passed away.

4. Prayer -- The Last Frontier of a Mature Christian

An exciting time in American history was when America was being settled by pioneers. Brave people left the comforts of home and headed West in covered wagons for the promise of a better life. They were daring, courageous and desperate. These pioneers envisioned going to places they had never been before. They were tired of the ordinary, the status quo.

Another word describes this era. It concerns their destination -- **the frontier**. A frontier refers to an undeveloped area. A frontier means new, **uncharted territory** where no one has ever been.

> "A frontier is that part of a country that is unexplored or undeveloped. Any new field of learning, thought, etc. or any part of a field that is incompletely investigated, e.g. a frontier of medicine, aviation or technology."[1]

183

Doctors are constantly exploring the frontier of medicine. The boundaries of aviation and computer technology are constantly being pushed and expanded by innovators.

A spiritual frontier refers to:
- New territory -- places we have never been in the Spirit and in our relationship with God.
- Experiencing the battlefield and harvest field beyond our prior involvement.

The last frontier to be conquered by the mature Christian is not the world, the flesh or the devil; these allude to defending ourselves against their forces. The frontier concept requires moving on the offense. It is pushing to the edge, experiencing the **bleeding leading edge of sacrifice and self-denial.** It involves going where we have never been in God's Kingdom to more effectively reach the lost.

- **The mature Christian conquers the last frontier by following the unbeaten path into new territory (the supernatural) through the doorway of prayer.**

Prayer fuels the engine of our relationship with God. Without it, our spiritual man will decline. We must consciously choose to spend time with God every day in prayer. Unlimited distractions such as hobbies, entertainment, education, career, material possessions, friends, family, and overcrowded secular schedules cause prayer to be neglected.

While by themselves, they may not be sin; they become sin when crowding prayer out of our lives. This may include being too involved in the Martha ministry vs. the Mary ministry -- doing good things, including Christian service, to the exclusion of the best things, kneeling at the feet of Jesus.

It involves a cycle of, "being" *(transformation)* before "doing" *(dominion)*.

Special blessings result when we retreat to a solitary place, like Jesus, for a time of daily prayer. It is a sacrifice of the will, an act of discipline; it is work.

Mark 1:35 Jesus, our example in prayer.
And in the morning, rising up a great while before day, he went out, and departed into a solitary place, and there prayed.

Luke 6:12
And it came to pass in those days, that he went out into a mountain to pray, and continued all night in prayer to God.

-- From "E. M. Bounds"

The people who have done the most for God in this world have been early on their knees. He who fritters away the early morning, its opportunity and its freshness, in other pursuits than seeking God will make poor headway seeking him the rest of the day. If God is not first in our thoughts and efforts in the morning, he will be in the last place the remainder of the day.[2]

Satan assaults us daily at our prayer closet door. He challenges our decision to spend good quality time talking to God in prayer. He will convince us that with our busy schedule we do not have time. But God will give us back that time, and more, if we seek Him first. Refer to Appendix 4 for a summary of some misconceptions regarding prayer.

The story is told about Napoleon and his generals on one of their expeditions. From the maps, they disagreed on where they were located. Finally, Napoleon stood up and announced:

"Gentlemen we have just marched off the maps, we are somewhere we have never been, we are in uncharted territory."

To experience the frontier, we must leave our comfort zones and march off the maps into God's Kingdom where we have never been before. This involves crossing Jordan into God's promises of the supernatural, leaving behind unproductive efforts in the wilderness. The challenge is new territory, new victories, and new anointing in our lives (divine ability vs. our ability).

A **natural frontier** denotes sacrifice -- giving up the familiar with its ease and comfort, traveling difficult trails, and often death. A **spiritual frontier** also requires sacrifice -- prayer, fasting, purity, service, and death of the carnal man. This will take us to new levels in our relationship with God, giving new levels of dominion to do His work.

We face impossible problems, pressures, and predicaments. But, on our knees we find wisdom and guidance for difficult decisions, power for challenging situations and love for people that are mistreating us. The greatest source of internal power is prayer.

Prayer is work. Prayer is sometimes intense and difficult – fighting through the hindrances of Satan and self. Effective prayer brings submission of our will to His. Prayer changes things as well as the heart of the person who prays.

Jesus set the example for prayer. Prayer was His life; His life was prayer. Prayer was the source of power and guidance for Jesus, as the Son of man, to fulfill His mission. More than twenty times the Gospels call attention to Jesus in prayer. Jesus clearly emphasized that prayer was important and mandatory for the Christian when He said in, *Matt. 6:5, Mark 11:25*, and *Luke 11:2, "**When ye pray**", not "If you pray."*

-- From "Matthew Henry's Commentary"

"When thou prayest" (v. 5). It is taken for granted that all the disciples of Christ pray. As soon as Paul was converted, behold he prayeth. You may as soon find a living man that does not breathe, as a living Christian that does not pray. For this shall every one that is godly pray. If prayerless, then graceless.[3]

Before Jesus, as Son of man, touched the sick and lonely, He first touched the throne of God. Before He displayed power, He received it. A private victory alone in prayer precedes a public victory. There must be a private anointing before there is a public anointing. When we pray in private, we will have power in public.

What was true for Jesus is especially true for us. There are no "secrets" to power. The "secret" is found in a solitary place alone with God. If we invest in prayer, we will reap the dividend in power.

What was the most difficult time for Jesus at the end of His ministry? Was it praying in the Garden of Gethsemane, or was it His suffering on the cross? Studying the various Gospel accounts, we see Him struggling in prayer in the Garden, fighting through His human fear and will. Praying was difficult; His sweat was like great drops of blood. He spent the night in prayer on Mount Olivet praying with strong crying and tears: *"Who in the days of his flesh, when he had offered up prayers and supplications with **strong crying and tears** unto him that was able to save him from death" (Heb. 5:7).*

Jesus won the victory in the Garden. He received strength to endure the most cruel and painful death on the cross. On the cross, He calmly spoke peace to those around Him. When the most difficult test came, He had already gained the victory through prayer.

If Jesus needed this kind of praying to face His greatest trial, how much more we need to pray. Jesus knew He must finish His work; and to do so, He prayed fervently, consistently, and persistently.

If we are to conquer a new frontier in the Spirit; if we are to finish the work that He has entrusted to us, we must pray like Jesus. We must pray the prayer of Jesus in the Garden: *"Nevertheless not as I will, but as thou wilt"* -- not my will, but thy will be done.

We can remain at the first level of prayer -- seeking God's hands. This is praying only when we are in trouble. If that is the only time we will pray, God may continue sending problems to keep us talking to Him. Or we can move to a higher level of prayer, maintaining a consistent and balanced prayer life (relationship prayer, transformation prayer and dominion prayer.

E. M. Bounds said: "The crying evils of these times, maybe of all times is little or no praying. Of these two evils, perhaps little praying is worse than no praying. Little praying is a kind of a salve for the conscience."

The highest calling is the call to prayer -- regardless of our place of ministry in God's Kingdom, our efforts will only be successful with prayer. The transition between Law and Grace was accomplished by prayer -- Jesus' prayer alone in the Garden. His request to His disciples was: ***"Could you not***

watch* (pray) *with me one hour? Watch and pray, that ye enter not into temptation: the spirit indeed is willing, but the flesh is weak" (Matt. 26:40, 41).

Today we are in the transition between the dispensation of Grace and the end of the age which will usher in the Millennial Reign of Jesus Christ. Jesus repeats the same question today: ***"Could you not watch* (pray) *with me one hour"?***

One reason we may struggle so much with prayer is that results are not always immediate. King David said, *"I waited patiently for the Lord and he inclined his ear."* Isaiah wrote, *"They that wait upon the Lord shall renew their strength."*

Rev. T. F. Tenney said, "We live in a microwave society. We want instant results, but we have a crock pot God. Sometimes it seems that God moves slowly, but His answer always comes on time."

We can use prayer like a checking account -- hurrying to make a deposit to cover the check. Or, we can use prayer like a savings account, making systematic, regular deposits assuring a positive balance to draw from in times of need. Consistent prayer in time of peace builds a shelter for protection in time of storm.

Prayer can be compared to a chemist adding one drop of a chemical to a solution without results. Then he adds another drop and another . . . and finally one last drop. Suddenly everything immediately changes -- a chemical reaction takes place. Was it the last drop that caused the change? No, it was a culmination of all the drops.

In Acts, Chapter 10, Cornelius prayed day 1, day 2, day 100, day 200, perhaps 999 days or longer. Then suddenly an angel appeared with instructions to send for apostle Peter, who would reveal the plan of salvation. Was it his last prayer? Again, it was the culmination of many prayers. It was a tipping point, when the bowl overflowed and the answer came pouring out. The angel said, ***"Your prayers have come up as a memorial"***. God could not ignore his prayers.

In the Old Testament, we see this concept in the two prayers of Elijah. At Mount Carmel, when Elijah concluded praying a sixty-four word prayer, there came an immediate and miraculous answer from God: *"Then the fire of the Lord fell, and consumed the burnt sacrifice, and the wood, and the stones, and the dust, and licked up the water that was in the trench" (1 Kings 18:38).*

But on Mount Carmel, when Elijah prayed for rain, the answer did not come immediately. Before his answer came, he prayed seven times and sent his servant to go up and look toward the sea seven times. Elijah just kept praying because he knew it was God's promised time for rain. He prayed for hours until the answer came.

Do not be discouraged when your prayers are not answered immediately. Keep building a memorial of prayers to God until the answer comes.

Breakthrough in a Natural Frontier

As a team working on a breakthrough in technology, medicine, etc., senses they are close to a solution, something happens to them. They become more intense, losing interest in everything else. With only one thing on their mind, they cancel all other plans and work longer hours. As they get closer to the solution, a synergy and unity forms within the team members. This intensity propels them beyond their own individual abilities. They persist until the breakthrough has been accomplished.

It is time for the endtime church and Christian to experience a breakthrough in the spiritual frontier -- a breakthrough into restoration of apostolic ministry as recorded in the book of Acts. This will happen when we match the dedication and unity of the teams working on secular frontiers such as medicine and technology. We must become more intense until nothing else is on our mind except achieving a breakthrough that will deliver and save many souls. At stake, is deliverance of millions bound in prisons of sin, abuse, drugs, alcohol, despair, and hopelessness.

A Frontier - Walking on the Moon

In 1960, President J. F. Kennedy made the famous statement, "We choose to go to the moon, not because it is easy, but because it is hard." There were numerous difficulties to overcome, including complex technical problems to solve because no one had ever done this before.

Amazingly, this project team caught the vision of putting a rocket into space and landing on the moon. An incredible amount of synergy developed within the team because they were all focused on one thing -- putting a man on the moon.

Working late one night, one of the men said, "Have you noticed the change in the whole team working on this project? Something has happened to us. Look how we figured out a solutions to complicated problems. Our team has accomplished things we never dreamed would be possible. What do you think has caused this?"

Bill, pointing to the sky remarked, "See that moon up there?

Men have wondered about it for years, but we are getting ready to go there. That is what has changed us. We believe we can go to a place where no one has been before -- conquering a new frontier."

May we have that kind of passion and vision to go in the Spirit where we have never been. Catching that kind of vision and fervent prayer will change us as we pursue a breakthrough in a frontier of the Kingdom. What moon do we want to walk on in the Spirit? What do we want to experience for the first time -- what frontier? "Oh God, let us catch a vision of the frontier where You are calling us -- to experience a breakthrough that will make a difference in our community and our world."

A trailblazer on the frontier of God's Kingdom will be a:
- **Discoverer of new heights and depths in the Spirit.**
- **Seeker of greater revelation of God and His ways.**
- **Passionate man driven by the purpose and will of God.**
- **Disciplined man driven to a consistent Christian life of prayer and service.**

5. Conclusion

5.1 The Challenge

The challenge we face as a church and born-again believers in these momentous times is four-fold: (a) the gigantic overwhelming size of the harvest, (b) the unprecedented forces of evil that Satan has marshalled and set in array to attack the church, (c) the shortness of time, (d) the shortage of laborers working in the harvest.

(a) Size of the Harvest

There is an ever-increasing population on the earth to reach with the gospel. As of 2016, the world population is 7.5 billion. That is 25 times more people than were in the world at the time of Jesus Christ. To match the results in the book of Acts, we must experience a revival in our world 25 times greater.

	Birth Rate	Death Rate	Increase
Year	131,400,000	55,300,000	76,100
Day	360,000	151,600	208,400
Hour	15,000	6,316	8,684
Minute	250	105	145
Second	4	1.75	2.25

(b) The unprecedented forces of evil that Satan has marshalled and set in array to attack the church

Corrupt and perverted conditions are rising in our nation and world at an alarming rate. Satan is leading a revival of wickedness with more sin, abuse, sickness and perversion than any prior generation. The affluence and prosperity of our society is fighting against the mission and vision of the church. This spirit of the Antichrist is rapidly increasing in the world and challenging the church on every front:

- The Supreme Court has redefined the biblical definition of marriage and changed the laws of the U.S. to support same sex marriage.

- The LGBT agenda is being pushed at every level from the Supreme Court and the president (2015) in the White House, to the city government and local school districts. Speaking out against sin defined in the Bible is a hate crime in some countries and will soon be in the U.S.

- Lawlessness, with rebellion and hatred toward the law and lawmen, is rising at an unprecedented rate in our country. Examples of this include: city officials illegally refusing to obey federal law to detain and deport illegal immigrants that have committed felonies; organizations formed that disrespect, demonize and encourage the killing of police officers, who are commissioned to keep us safe.

- Terrorism in every part of the world with airplanes being blown out of the sky, suicide bombers, major attacks on innocent people in public places, etc. – wars and rumors of wars threatening the start of a global conflict (World War III prophesied to kill one-third of mankind).

May we, as born-again believers, respond with increased dominion and authority over this evil spirit of the Antichrist rapidly rising in the world today.

The final battle between right and wrong, between the forces of good and evil, will be even more violent because it is Satan's final stand to destroy the purpose of God for the last great harvest of lost souls. Our adversary, the devil, will not attack the believer with temptations of the flesh and obvious sin. He will work in a subtle way to get us to relax; to get distracted; to be at ease in Zion; to become self-centered and entertainment-centered; to do our own will vs. doing God's will.

(c) The Shortness of Time

We are working in the endtime -- in the late evening shadows of 6,000 years of man's day. We are standing on the brink of eternity with the task of reaching a generation that is further from God than any prior one. This seemingly impossible task, to reach the lost souls of this godless, hopeless generation, with time running out, demands a revival of fervent apostolic prayer. No other resource will substitute for prayer to invoke the operation of the supernatural required for victory against our vicious adversary. If the church is to meet the needs of a desperate world, with time running out, we must pursue a supernatural course of action driven by fervent and balanced prayer.

Rom. 13:11, 12
*11 And that **knowing the time**, that now it is high time to awake out of sleep; for now is our salvation nearer than when we believed.*
12 The night is far spent, the day is at hand; let us therefore cast off the works of darkness and let us put on the amour of light.

11 But make sure that you don't get so absorbed and exhausted in taking care of all your day-by-day obligations that you lose track of the time and doze off, oblivious to God. 12 The night is about over, dawn is about to break. Be up and awake to what God is doing! **BCL**

"And that knowing the time" - There are three things that tell us about prophetic time: the Bible, the calendar, and world news. These three sources are now in alignment like the sun, moon and earth in a total eclipse of the sun. These announce that we are at the end of the Church Age, just before the second coming of Jesus Christ.

It is the end of **time**! It is **time** to diligently seek Him in consistent and fervent prayer. It is **time** for dominion and restoration! It is harvest **time**!

- **It is time to expand our vision of the harvest field and what God wants to do in us and through us, in this last and final harvest.**

We still have time to reach lost souls. But if we don't respond to the urgency of the times, we may hear the sad reframe recoded by the prophet Jeremiah: *"The harvest is past, the summer is ended, and we are not saved.* **Is there no balm in Gilead; is there no physician there?***" (Jer. 8:20, 22)*

If we believe we are at the end of the Church Age and this is the last harvest season, then we must take the appropriate actions to ensure that we are giving our best efforts to the Father's Business.

(d) The Shortage of Laborers Working in the Harvest

This is discussed in the following sub-chapter, 5.3, "Jesus' Only Prayer Request."

5.2 The Answer to the Challenge

The answer to the challenge of the unfinished task is simply elevating the **mission, vision, goals** and the **core ministry** of the church to the highest level and priority. Doing this will move toward a **harvest driven church** vs. a maintenance driven church (defined in Chart L-5 of the Addendum Volume).

Refer to the following PowerPoint charts at the end of this chapter:

 C-1 Path to Dominion in the Supernatural through the Core Ministry of the Church.

 C-2 Prayer Ministry and Care Ministry.

 C-3 Reaping Your Personal Harvest Field.

 C-4 Core Ministry Organization Model Example.

Although the supporting ministries of the church are needed and important, they must not compete with the core ministry of the church -- the two arms of the church:

- **The Power Arm - Prayer Ministry**
  (reaching for more of Him).

- **The Actions Arm - Compassion and Care Ministry**
  (reaching for more of them).

(a) The Power Arm - Prayer Ministry

Prayer is the key that brings the anointing (divine ability) to effectively do God's work and fulfill the mission of the church -- *"Seeking and saving the lost"*. If we are to make significant improvements in our outreach efforts, we must have God's wisdom and anointing. Anointing comes with sacrifice, and sacrifice begins and ends with prayer.

Prayer is not a department of the church; it is the **power generator** of the church. The Prayer Ministry **must not** be perceived as just another ministry of the church; it must be elevated and presented as:

- The most important process in the church.
- The enabling power for all other ministries and departments to become effective.
- The ministry in which everyone feels compelled to participate.

(b) The Actions Arm - Compassion and Care Ministry
   (Attracting, Winning and Retaining -- making disciples)

Soul Winning is not a department of the church -- it is the **mission** of the church. Every department in the church should justify its existence based on its contribution to the mission of saving souls and establishing them in the Kingdom of God.

The Compassion and Care Ministry must be elevated and designed:

- As the mission of the church.
- To bring awareness that every believer is a minister.
- To help everyone become involved in ministering to the needs of the lost, the sick and the hurting.

Prayer and fasting will bring anointing to pursue our dominion role – doing God's will and work. Exercising our dominion role is required to bring restoration to the power and evangelism of the book of Acts.

- **To reap a large harvest of souls, we must sacrifice and prepare for a large harvest of souls. Our actions must match our vision. And when God sees our faith, He will partner with us to bring the results.**

- **Our church will reach its potential when everyone in the church reaches his or her potential. For everyone who does not get involved, there will be souls that will not be reached.**

5.3 Jesus' Only Prayer Request

Jesus identified the most significant hindrance to reaping the harvest when he declared: *"The laborers are few."*

Matt. 9:37, 38
37 Then saith he unto his disciples, The harvest truly is plenteous, but the labourers are few;
*38 **Pray ye therefore the Lord of the harvest, that he will send forth labourers into his harvest.***

38 So pray to the Lord who is in charge of the harvest; ask him to send more workers into his fields. NLT

- **The only prayer request that Jesus made during His entire ministry was simply that we would pray for more workers to be sent into the harvest field.**

When we consider that Jesus made only one prayer request during His entire earthly ministry, it should cause us to pause and seriously consider our response. This single request was a subject of utmost urgency and priority by Jesus and should be to us today. It was one so dear to the heart of the Master that after two millennia this message still rings out and calls for our commitment today. And may this urgent and powerful request by the Lord of the Harvest convict, and motivate us to answer the call to pray:

 - That laborers would be sent into the harvest.
 - That we would be one of those chosen and empowered to work in the endtime harvest.

When we study the preceding verses, we can understand some of what we may be doing when we are fulfilling His prayer request: *"And Jesus went about all the cities and villages, teaching in their synagogues, and preaching the Gospel of the kingdom, and healing every sickness and every disease among the people. But when he saw the multitudes, he was moved with compassion on them, because they fainted, and were scattered abroad, as sheep having no shepherds"* *(Matt. 9:35, 36).*

When I see a sinner in desperate need of deliverance and salvation, three words scream in my ear, "Calvary was enough" -- "Calvary was enough" -- "Calvary was enough." There was enough blood shed at Calvary to redeem all of mankind. There was enough forgiveness and love provided to save the entire world. There is no shortage of supply. There is merely a shortage of workers to flow the love and plan of God to those in need.

Many battles have been lost because supplies did not reach the front lines. The enemy's strategy is to cut the supply line and keep the supply source from reaching the need. May we all be a part of the supply line to flow God's love and compassion and message of hope to our lost world.

-- From "Jesus' Prayer Request"

What if Jesus came to you with a prayer request? Would you pray for it? Jesus made only one prayer request during His ministry. It is found in Matthew 9:38 and Luke 10:2: ***"Pray ye therefore the Lord of the harvest, that he would send forth labourers into his harvest."***

When was the last time you prayed for Jesus' request? The problem for some in praying for this request is they don't want to be a laborer. How can I pray that prayer if I'm not willing to become a laborer myself?

I find it interesting that the only prayer request Jesus ever made was for people to be committed in the harvest of lost souls! That should show how important it is to Him! How important is it to you? Will you be an answer to His prayer request?[1]

Are we polishing our ticket to heaven by validating it every Sunday with a religious routine? Or are we sharpening our sword for the battle and our sickle for the harvest? The relevant message for the born-again Christian is not to prepare for the rapture, but to prepare for the battle and harvest. Because if we are involved in the His business we will be ready for the rapture. Refer to PowerPoint Chart C-3, "Reaping Your Personal Harvest Field", at the end of this chapter.

The first battle is not against demons and the kingdom of Satan; it is against carnality, apathy and self:

- Self-will vs. God's will.
- Our mind vs. the mind of Christ.
- Our limited human love vs. Christ's love and compassion for a lost world.

The purpose of the PowerPoint charts on the following pages is to highlight the core ministry of the church and depict the dependence of the actions arm (Compassion and Care Ministry) of the church on the power arm (Prayer Ministry) of the church.

Chart	PowerPoint Chart Name and Comments
C-1	**The Path to Dominion in the Supernatural Through the Core Ministry of the Church** Although the supporting ministries are needed and important, the core ministry of the church involves the Power Arm (Prayer Ministry) and the Actions Arm (Care Ministry: Attract, Win, Retain, and Make Disciples).
C-2	**Prayer Ministry and Care Ministry** The depth of our dominion (actions) in the harvest field is directly related to the depth of our relationship with God which is related to our depth in prayer.
C-3	**Reaping Your Personal Harvest Field** Just as Abraham's servant was led by God to find a bride for Isaac, God's Spirit will lead us into the harvest field to find those who will complete His bride.
C-4	**The Front Door of the Care Room is the Back Door of the Care Room** The effectiveness of the Care Ministry (attracting, winning, retaining and making disciples) is dependent on the effectiveness of the Prayer Ministry.
C-5	**Revival and Evangelism Through the Two Arms of the Church** Revival is the result of the moving of the Spirit of God. Organization and planning are only used to facilitate the saint's involvement, enhance the effectiveness and retain the results.
C-6	**Revival of the Saint and Evangelism of the Sinner** Both of these involve the two critical areas of Prayer Ministry and the Care Ministry.
C-7	**Core Ministry Org. Model Example** This identifies the various potential functions of the Core Ministry. This is a general example that can be used for discussion purposes to create the unique core ministry needed for a particular church.

Conclusion

Chart C-1

THE PATH TO DOMINION IN THE SUPERNATURAL

Through the Core Ministry of the Church

The Only Hope For Reaching **This Lost End-time Generation**

PASSION

C H U R C H

Mandatory Involvement *Optional Involvement*

1.
CORE MINISTRY:

2.
SUPPORTING MINISTRIES:

> **SOUL WINNING** (Mission)
  Fulfilling the "Great Commission"
  Healing, Deliverance, Salvation
> **PRAYER** and the **WORD** (Power)
  (Spirit. . . . and . . . Truth)

THE TWO MINISTRIES:
  THE PRAYER MINISTRY (Passion)
  THE CARE MINISTRY (Compassion)

THE TWO ARMS OF THE CHURCH:
  The Power Arm
  The Actions Arm

- Physical Operation & Organization
- Choir   - Music
- Drama   - Ushers
- Clerical   - Other Helps, etc.

These supporting ministries are needed and
important. It is a wonderful thing when natural
giftings are dedicated and anointed of God and used
in His kingdom. But they must never be substituted
for the mission of the church enabled by spiritual
gifting and divine ability. Our responsibility to fulfill
the "Great Commission to Win the Lost" is not
discharged through our natural talents and giftings.
Nowhere in Holy Scripture do we find God working
through man's talents, abilities or natural giftings to
perform His supernatural work.

PASSION BRINGS POWER

Born Again Believer

God's eternal purpose
and will for every
born-again believer is to
<u>fulfill the great commission</u>
to work in His harvest field
reaching lost souls.

This is a **Spiritual Work**
and will not be done
with natural talents and
giftings. This will almost
always be misaligned with
The natural man's desires,
abilities and comfort zone.

SPIRITUAL MAN	NATURAL MAN	
Son of God	Son of Man	
SPIRIT	**SOUL**	**BODY**
Supernatural Gifting	- WILL - MIND - EMOTIONS	THE FIVE SENSES
Divine Ability Vs Man's Ability	**Natural** - Gifting - Ability - Talent	

This will always involve:
 - His Will Vs Our Will (Not Our Choice but His)
 - His Thinking Vs Our Thinking (His ways)
 - His Emotions Vs Our Emotions (Deep sorrow
   for their suffering with a strong urge to help)

Power

*Zech. 4:6-7 You will not succeed by
your own strength, but by my Spirit.
Obstacles as great as mountains will
disappear before you. TEV*

Chart C-2

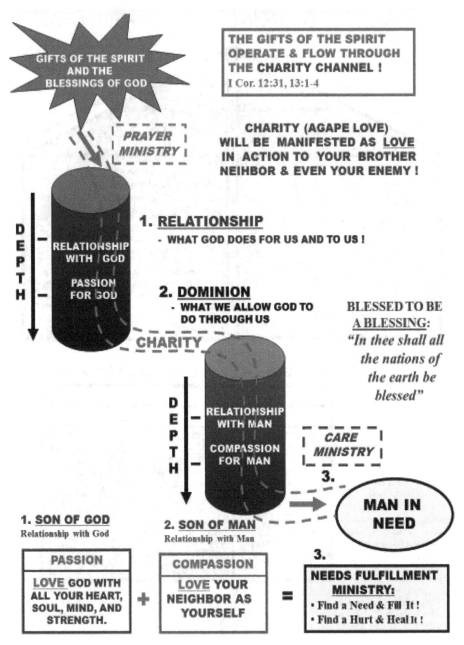

THE GIFTS OF THE SPIRIT
OPERATE & FLOW THROUGH
THE **CHARITY** CHANNEL !
I Cor. 12:31, 13:1-4

GIFTS OF THE SPIRIT
AND THE
BLESSINGS OF GOD

**PRAYER
MINISTRY**

CHARITY (AGAPE LOVE)
WILL BE MANIFESTED AS <u>LOVE</u>
IN ACTION TO YOUR BROTHER
NEIHBOR & EVEN YOUR ENEMY !

D
E
P
T
H

RELATIONSHIP
WITH GOD

PASSION
FOR GOD

1. RELATIONSHIP
- WHAT GOD DOES FOR US AND TO US !

2. DOMINION
- WHAT WE ALLOW GOD TO
DO THROUGH US

BLESSED TO BE
A BLESSING:
*"In thee shall all
the nations of
the earth be
blessed"*

CHARITY

D
E
P
T
H

RELATIONSHIP
WITH MAN

COMPASSION
FOR MAN

**CARE
MINISTRY**

3.

**MAN IN
NEED**

1. SON OF GOD
Relationship with God

2. SON OF MAN
Relationship with Man

3.

PASSION	COMPASSION	NEEDS FULFILLMENT MINISTRY:
<u>LOVE</u> GOD WITH ALL YOUR HEART, SOUL, MIND, AND STRENGTH.	<u>LOVE</u> YOUR NEIGHBOR AS YOURSELF	• Find a Need & Fill It ! • Find a Hurt & Heal It !

+ =

Chart C-3

REAPING YOUR PERSONAL HARVEST FIELD

WHEN WE DO OUR PART – GOD WILL BACK US UP & DO HIS PART

STIR UP THE GIFT THAT IS IN YOU !

- Exercising Faith – Repetition
- Dominion Prayer for the Harvest
- Experiencing His Will & Work
- Believing that God Needs You
- Feeling His Passion - Compassion
- Envisioning a Mega Harvest
- Claiming a Double Portion
- Partnering with God to do His Work
- Following Jesus' Example and
  Approach to Soul Winning

THERE IS ANGELIC HELP IN REAPING THE HARVEST! Heb. 1:14

Soul Winning is a <u>Spiritual Process</u> - Led by the Spirit:

- The greater depth of our relationship with God, the greater depth and effectiveness of our dominion role in the harvest (attracting, winning and retaining).

LET YOUR LIGHT SO SHINE -
In Every Dark Place:

- You are the lamp
- He is the source of all light
- Walk in the light as He is in the light and it will shine thru you

LIGHT OF REVELATION TO US:

- God's will for our life
- As a son of God our purpose is to duplicate the ministry of Jesus, that He exampled to us on earth as the Son of God

HIS LIGHT SHINING THRU US -
To a Dark & Hurting World:
His light will direct you to those that shall be heirs of salvation:

- They will be changed
- You will be changed

GOD'S GLORY & LIGHT

LED BY THE SPIRIT INTO THE HARVEST FIELD!

The wise men were led by a light to Jesus.
Abraham's servant was led by God to find a bride for Isaac.
As many as are led by the Spirit, they are the sons of God.
The Spirit will lead us into the harvest field (finding a bride for Christ).

His light will direct our steps in the harvest field !

The Center of God's Will is the Harvest Field

The meeting place for the rapture is the harvest field !

Chart C-4

THE FRONT DOOR OF THE CARE ROOM

IS THE BACK DOOR OF THE PRAYER ROOM

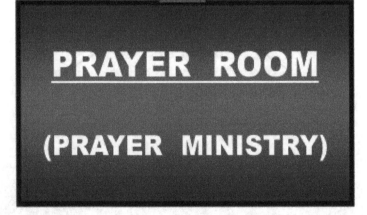

Chart C-5

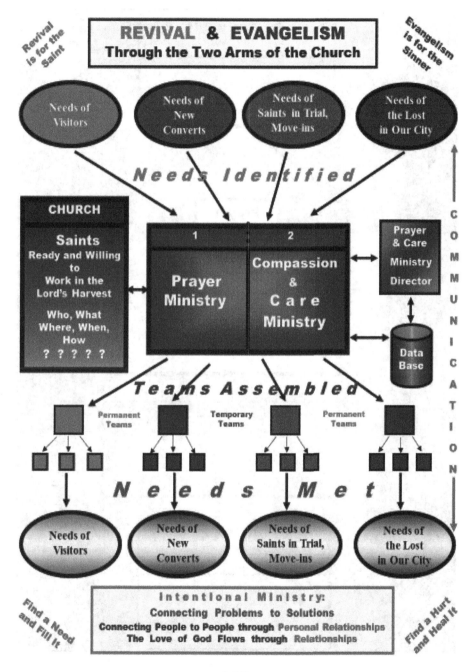

Revival is for the Saint

Evangelism is for the Sinner

REVIVAL & EVANGELISM
Through the Two Arms of the Church

Needs of Visitors

Needs of New Converts

Needs of Saints in Trial, Move-ins

Needs of the Lost in Our City

Needs Identified

CHURCH

Saints
Ready and Willing to Work in the Lord's Harvest

Who, What Where, When, How
? ? ? ? ?

1
Prayer Ministry

2
Compassion & Care Ministry

Prayer & Care Ministry Director

Data Base

COMMUNICATION

Teams Assembled

Permanent Teams

Temporary Teams

Permanent Teams

Needs Met

Needs of Visitors

Needs of New Converts

Needs of Saints in Trial, Move-ins

Needs of the Lost in Our City

Find a Need and Fill It

Find a Hurt and Heal It

Intentional Ministry:
Connecting Problems to Solutions
Connecting People to People through Personal Relationships
The Love of God Flows through Relationships

Chart C-6

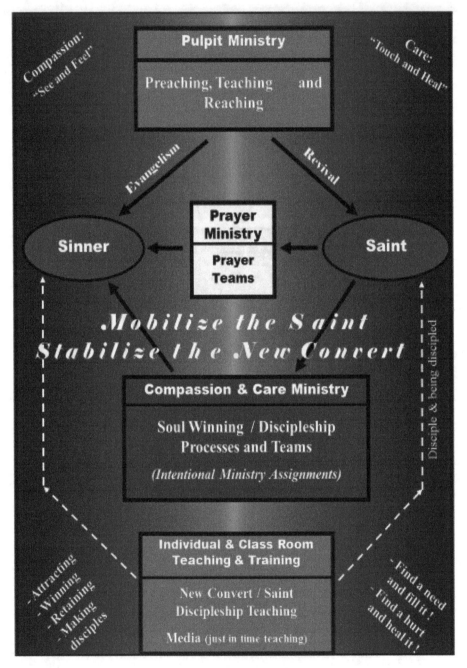

Chart C-7

PRAYER MINISTRY: FOCUS: Provide a prayer covering for all the Care Ministry Teams and needs.   ORG: 4 Prayer Teams of 40 each (for a church of 160 members)

— COMPASSION & CARE MINISTRY —
NEEDS DRIVEN — MINISTERING TO NEEDS

1. ATTRACTING

COMMUNITY CARE MINISTRY

FOCUS:
People with self-confessed needs in the saints' circle of influence outside the church walls. Making friends, building relation-ships, and ministering first to the physical needs (outer court) of sinners.

ORG:
- Individual level (All)
- Team level (SWAT Team)
Ministering to the hurting (e.g. homeless and hospitals)

2. WINNING

CRITICAL CARE TEAM MINISTRY

FOCUS:
Two-on-one Care for visitors 4 week follow-up and ministry to their needs.
ORG: 4 Care Teams (4 - 5 on each team)

HOSPITALITY SUITE

FOCUS: Visitor reception drinks / snacks & fellowship with Care Team and Pastor.

- Home Bible Study
- New Converts Class, etc.

3. RETAINING

MENTOR CARE MINISTRY

FOCUS: 1 year 1-on-1 Care for visitors & new converts.

DISCIPLESHIP CARE MINISTRY

FOCUS: New Converts Training: Home Bible Studies, New Converts Class, etc.

HOME FELLOWSHIP CARE MINISTRY

FOCUS: Sinners & New Converts: Fellowship, Food. Ministry to individual needs

6. My Prayer

Oh Lord, our Lord, how excellent is Thy name in all the earth -- there is none like You!

We pray for the world that You bled and died for -- that You loved with an everlasting love. We pray for world leaders to have wisdom to seek peace, with justice for all. We pray for our country, our president and our congressional leaders to have wisdom and unity to make the right decisions for our nation and world.

We pray for Israel and for peace in that ancient land. We pray for Jerusalem, because Your Word instructs us to, "pray for the peace of Jerusalem" -- the birthplace of the church. We pray for the resolution of conflict between Israel and the Palestinians. We pray for those involved in the conflict, and the world leaders seeking a solution for peace.

We pray for every nation experiencing the tragedy of war. With all the violence and turmoil, these nations need our prayers more than ever. We pray for the safety of our armed forces and others trying to maintain peace in these war-torn countries.

We pray for the victims of worldwide violence and war, for those wounded in body and in mind. We pray for the multitudes of refugees forced from their homes.

We pray for the peace of those separated by war and those bereaved for family members fallen in battle. We pray for the release of prisoners of war.

We pray against the dark forces of terrorism. We pray against the organizations and individuals who are attempting to wreak havoc and create fear. We bind demons and spirits of terrorism that would disrupt peace and hinder the work of the gospel around the world.

We are deeply aware of the tragic cycle of continuing violence around the world. We pray for the suffering, and we pray against those responsible for it. Let the peace of God flow through our churches to heal ancient grudges and bitter hatreds that have imprisoned people for many generations.

We pray for those living in famine-ravaged areas, for children and adults starving for natural and spiritual bread. We pray for social justice and the healing of crippling poverty affecting millions of people living in misery and hopelessness.

We pray for the children and orphans around the world who are homeless, hungry and hurting.

We pray for world peace. Dear Jesus, we pray for Your peace to rule in our world:

- If there is to be peace in the world,
    there must be peace in the nations.

- If there is to be peace in the nations,
    there must be peace in the cities.

- If there is to be peace in the cities,
    there must be peace between neighbors.

- If there is to be peace between neighbors,
    there must be peace in the home.

- If there is to be peace in the home,
    there must be peace in the heart.

"May the peace of God that passes all understanding keep our hearts and minds through Christ Jesus" (Phil. 4:7).

We pray for physical and spiritual needs -- worldwide revival and evangelism. As surely as physical wars exist throughout the world, there are spiritual battles of greater proportions. In the name of Jesus, we bind every power of Satan that would hinder revival and evangelism.

Give us revival and evangelism in every region of the world:
    - North and South America
    - Central America and the Caribbean
    - Africa
    - Pacific
    - Europe and the Middle East
    - Asia

Grant us favor with government officials and people of these nations that we can effectively reach them with the gospel.

We pray for the persecuted believers in North Korea, China, India, Vietnam, Indonesia, Pakistan, Malaysia, Sri Lanka and other places in the world. Give them strength and encouragement to endure and stand firm in their faith.

213

Let us be aware every day of the unfinished task and that time is expiring. Place us in the center of Your will to accomplish everything You intended us to accomplish in Your Kingdom – in Your harvest field. Grant us dominion, power and authority over Satan and sickness.

We pray the darkness and deception of Satan's kingdom will be overwhelmed by the light of Your glorious gospel. Drive back the power of the Antichrist that would hinder the gospel and Your Kingdom work. Above all, we pray for great endtime revival and evangelism where many laborers answer the call of the harvest.

We pray against apathy and the lukewarm spirit of the age that would dull our awareness of Your soon coming and a lost world that desperately needs You. Don't let us be satisfied with the usual, the routine, or the status quo. Let us be awake, vigilant, working and doing Your will. Help us to put on the whole armor of God, engaging in battle against the kingdom of darkness. Help us reach spiritual frontiers where we have never been before.

Dear God, let us see like You see. Heal us of our spiritual myopia, which causes our vision to be blurred and nearsighted. Open the windows of our minds, expand our thinking and let us understand what You intended for us to be and do when You said: *"Lift up your eyes, and look on the fields; for they are white already to harvest."*

Thank You for the "burning bush" experiences when Your awesome manifested presence has touched our lives. But let us now become the burning bush -- set on fire with a passion driven by Your love.

My Prayer

When the last rays of light have faded on this final generation and Your great time clock of the ages has expired, let us be found pursuing Your business, with a sword in one hand and a sickle in the other, fighting in Your battle and working in Your harvest.

We humbly pray for these things. We pray because of the hope within us and because we love You and lost souls throughout the world.

Jesus, we thank You today that Your light directs us, Your love surrounds us and Your power strengthens us.

And last but not least help us to develop a more powerful and balanced prayer life that will empower us to be more effective in Your harvest field and battlefield.

Thank You for hearing and answering our prayer.

In the precious name of Jesus, amen.

IV. Appendices

Appendix 1
Prayer Scriptures

1. Prayers are Permanent Assets That Live Until the End of Time

Prayers are not temporary; they are permanent assets stored somewhere in God's kingdom until the end of time. The prayers of the saints live on, even after their death. The lips that uttered them may be closed in death, and the heart that felt them may have ceased to beat, but prayers outlive a generation, outlive a millennia and outlive a world. Many mother's prayers for a lost child have been answered after her death. And her prayers have made the difference in the lives of a family for generations after her death.

God places such high value on our prayers that He has stored every sincere prayer we have prayed in a golden vial in heaven. *Rev. 5:8: "And when he had taken the book the four and twenty elders fell down before the lamb, having everyone of them harps, and golden vials full of odors, which are the prayers of the saints."* The prayers of the saints are precious to God. He records them and remembers them. Cornelius' prayers came up as a memorial to God and an angel was dispatched from heaven with a message of salvation.

219

2. Examples of Prayer That Jesus Set for Us

In his book, "Ordering Your Private World", Gordon MacDonald says that: "Prayer was such a priority to Jesus Christ that there are more than twenty words in the New Testament to describe His prayer life. This habitual drawing aside, alone in a solitary place to pray, is vividly described by every Gospel writer."

Although we should have an attitude of prayer as we go about our daily activities (traveling in our car, etc.), is it necessary to have a private place and time of prayer? We see this exampled in the life of Jesus and His instruction to His disciples: *"When thou prayest, enter into your prayer closet and shut the door" (Matt. 6:6).*

Matt. 14:23
*And when he had sent the multitudes away, he went up into a **mountain apart to pray**: and when the evening was come, he was there alone.*

Matt. 26:39
*And he **went a little further, and fell on his face, and prayed**, saying, O my Father, if it be possible, let this cup pass from me: nevertheless not as I will, but as thou wilt.*

Mark 1:35
*And in the **morning, rising up a great while before day, he went out, and departed into a solitary place, and there prayed.***

Mark 6:46
*And when he had sent them away, he **departed into a mountain to pray.***

Luke 5:16
*And he **withdrew himself into the wilderness**, and prayed.*

Luke 6:12, 13 **(Before making an important decision Jesus prayed all night.)**
*12 And it came to pass in those days, that he **went out into a mountain to pray, and continued all night in prayer to God.**
13 And when it was day, he called unto him his disciples: and of them he chose twelve, whom also he named apostles;*

Luke 9:28, 29
*28 And it came to pass about an eight days after these sayings, he took Peter and John and James, and **went up into a mountain to pray.**
29 And as he prayed, the fashion of his countenance was altered, and his raiment was white and glistering.*

John 6:15
*When Jesus therefore perceived that they would come and take him by force, to make him a king, **he departed again into a mountain himself alone.***

3. Teaching People to Pray

The disciples of Jesus asked Him to teach them to pray and He responded to their request. There is great value in training people who are struggling with their daily devotional prayer life, particularly children and new converts.

Luke 11:1 **(The disciples ask Jesus to teach them to pray.)**
*And it came to pass, that, as he was praying in a certain place, when he ceased, one of his disciples said unto him, **Lord, teach us to pray, as John also taught his disciples.***

Matt. 6:6-11, 13, 14 **(Jesus teaching His disciples to pray.)**
*6 But thou, when thou prayest, **enter into thy closet**, and when thou hast shut thy door, pray to thy Father which is in secret; and thy Father which seeth in secret shall reward thee openly.*
7 But when ye pray, use not vain repetitions, as the heathen do: for they think that they shall be heard for their much speaking.
8 Be not ye therefore like unto them: for your Father knoweth what things ye have need of, before ye ask him.
9 After this manner therefore pray ye: Our Father which art in heaven, Hallowed be thy name.
10 Thy kingdom come. Thy will be done in earth, as it is in heaven.
11 Give us this day our daily bread. 12 And forgive us our debts, as we forgive our debtors.
13 And lead us not into temptation, but deliver us from evil: For thine is the kingdom, and the power, and the glory, forever. Amen.
14 For if ye forgive men their trespasses, your heavenly Father will also forgive you: But if ye forgive not men their trespasses, neither will your Father forgive your trespasses.

4. Disciples Praying in the Book of Acts Church

Acts 3:1, 2, 6-8 **(The first recorded miracle in the church was performed on the way to a prayer meeting.)**
*1 Now Peter and John went up together into the temple at the **hour of prayer,** being the ninth hour* (3:00 PM).
2 And a certain man lame from his mother's womb was carried, whom they laid daily at the gate of the temple which is called Beautiful, to ask alms of them that entered into the temple;

6 Then Peter said, Silver and gold have I none; but such as I have give I thee: In the name of Jesus Christ of Nazareth rise up and walk.

7 And he took him by the right hand, and lifted him up: and immediately his feet and ankle bones received strength.

8 And he leaping up stood, and walked, and entered with them into the temple, walking, and leaping, and praising God.

Acts 10:2-4, 9 **(The Gentiles were included in the plan of salvation because of prayer.)**

*2 A devout man, and one that feared God with all his house, which gave much alms to the people, and **prayed** to God always.*

*3 He saw in a vision evidently about the **ninth hour of the day** an angel of God coming in to him, and saying unto him, Cornelius.*

4 And when he looked on him, he was afraid, and said, What is it, Lord? And he said unto him, Thy prayers and thine alms are come up for a memorial before God.

*9 On the morrow, as they went on their journey, and drew nigh unto the city, Peter went up upon the housetop to **pray** about the sixth hour (noon):*

Acts 4:31

And when they had prayed, the place was shaken where they were assembled together; and they were all filled with the Holy Ghost, and they spake the word of God with boldness.

Acts 6:4 **(Emphasis on prayer by the ministry of the New Testament church.)**

But we will give ourselves continually to prayer, and to the ministry of the word.

223

Acts 6:6, 15
6 Whom they set before the apostles: and when they had prayed, they laid their hands on them.
15 Who, when they were come down, prayed for them, that they might receive the Holy Ghost:

Acts 9:40
But Peter put them all forth, and kneeled down, and prayed; and turning him to the body said, Tabitha, arise. And she opened her eyes: and when she saw Peter, she sat up.

Acts 12:5, 12
5 Peter therefore was kept in prison: but prayer was made without ceasing of the church unto God for him.
12 And when he had considered the thing, he came to the house of Mary the mother of John, whose surname was Mark; where many were gathered together praying.

Acts 16:25
And at midnight Paul and Silas prayed, and sang praises unto God: and the prisoners heard them.

Acts 22:17, 18 **(God warns Paul, while in prayer, to leave Jerusalem.)**
17 And it came to pass, that, when I was come again to Jerusalem, even while I prayed in the temple, I was in a trance;
18 And saw him saying unto me, Make haste, and get thee quickly out of Jerusalem: for they will not receive thy testimony concerning me.

Acts 28:8
And it came to pass, that the father of Publius lay sick of a fever and of a bloody flux: to whom Paul entered in, and prayed, and laid his hands on him, and healed him.

5. Scriptures Instructing Us to Pray

Luke 18:1
And he spake a parable unto them to this end, that men ought always to pray, and not to faint.

Luke 21:36
Watch ye therefore, and pray always, that ye may be accounted worthy to escape all these things that shall come to pass, and to stand before the Son of man.

Rom. 12:12
Rejoicing in hope; patient in tribulation; continuing instant in prayer.

Eph. 6:17, 18
17 And take the helmet of salvation, and the sword of the Spirit, which is the word of God:
18 Praying always with all prayer and supplication in the Spirit, and watching thereunto with all perseverance and supplication for all saints.

Phil. 4:6
Be careful for nothing; but in everything by prayer and supplication with thanksgiving let your requests be made known unto God.

Heb. 4:16
Let us therefore come boldly unto the throne of grace, that we may obtain mercy, and find grace to help in time of need.

1 Thess. 5:17
Pray without ceasing.

James 5:16, 17
*16 Confess your faults one to another, and pray one for another, that ye may be healed. **The effectual fervent prayer [powerful and effective] of a righteous man availeth much.** 17 Elias was a man subject to like passions as we are, and he prayed earnestly that it might not rain: and it rained not on the earth by the space of three years and six months.*

Appendix 2
Additional Books from the Author

Refer to the following pages for a brief description of each book in the eight volume progressive series entitled: **"I Must Be About My Father's Business"**:

Volume I
God's Purpose for Man
Relationship and Dominion

Volume I sets forth God's purpose for man -- relationship and dominion. It addresses in more depth man's **relationship** with God and God's desire to have a close and growing relationship with man.

This book discusses man sharing a mutual relationship of love, communication, and trust with God -- as a son of God, a friend of God, a servant of God and as the Bride of Christ. It also describes the God and man relationship roles: Father / Child, Groom / Bride, Friend / Friend, Master / Servant (love slave). It emphasizes God's **love** for man and man's love for God by loving his fellowman.

Volume II
Dominion
Doing God's Will and Work

This volume emphasizes the importance of **dominion**, since we often lead people to a relationship with God, but sometimes fail to help them take the next important step -- exercising dominion in the Kingdom of God. Dominion involves God sharing His authority and power with man in a partnership to fulfill His purpose and work on earth. The two concepts of relationship and dominion working together in a believer's life will bring balance, spiritual growth and fulfillment.

Love for God is the foundation for obedience which includes not just saying "no" to Satan and sin, but "yes" to God's perfect will for our lives.

This book addresses the subject of dominion and why we need to be involved in the mission and work of the Father's business. It includes many examples from both the Old and New Testaments of God's plan to work through man to accomplish His will on earth. It also describes God and man dominion roles: Great Physician / physician; Great High Priest / priest; Great Commander / soldier; King of kings / prince; Lord of the Harvest / harvester.

Volume III
Spiritual Growth – Passion for God
• Dominion Over Sin and Self

This book addresses **what** actions are required to become more effective in the Father's business. This encompasses foundational principles of spiritual growth that will prepare individuals to be more fruitful Christians. The primary emphasis is transformation: dominion over self (the will, the mind and the emotions) vs. dominion over sin.

Transformation is a continuous process of: less of my will and more of His, less of my thoughts and more of His, less of my limited human love and more of **God's perfect love**.

Spiritual growth results from a hunger and a passion for the things of God -- "Loving God with all of our heart, soul and mind." The will of God will always lead us to greater spiritual growth.

Spiritual growth at the individual level will result in church growth at the corporate level.

Volume IV
Unlimited Partnership
With a Supernatural God

The greatest reason for God's creation of man was that He might obtain sons to carry out His will and work on earth. He desired to reproduce His image in a creature.

The greatest reason for God's new creation of man (through a new birth, a spiritual birth) first recorded in the book of Acts, was that He might obtain **sons to carry out the supernatural work of His Kingdom**. True son-ship is an obligation to live out, or put in practice, the Father's nature. It is the Father's will for us as sons of God, to become, *"Partakers of His divine nature"*, His supernatural nature -- partnering with Him in His business.

As a partaker of the Father's divine nature we must grow in our **love** for God which will be manifested by our **love** and loving actions for man.

Volume V

Revival and Evangelism
- ## Passion for God
- ## Compassion for the Lost

The key to soul winning is **love** and compassion while exercising **dominion** in the harvest field.

This book describes some of the biblical foundational principles of revival and evangelism. Discussed in more detail is the "how to" of putting the evangelism principles into practice through the two arms of the church:

- The **Prayer Ministry** -- reaching for Him.

- The **Compassion and Care Ministry** (attracting, winning and retaining) -- reaching for them with God's **perfect love**.

Volume VI

Perfect Love

The Highest Law and Strongest Force

If we had only one word to describe God, it would be **"l-o-v-e."** If we had only one word to describe the entire Bible, it would be **"l-o-v-e"** -- a love story of God's love for mankind, a love letter to mankind.

- Love is the only motive accepted by God for working in His Kingdom . *"Though I have all spiritual gifts . . . give all my goods to the poor ... give my body to be burned, and have not love, it is nothing" (1 Cor. 13:1-3).*

- It is the foundation and driving force for everything that is meaningful and lasting in the Kingdom of God. It is the currency of God's Kingdom.

- It is the key element required to produce revival and evangelism with miracles, signs, and church growth, like the first century church in the book of Acts that shook their known world.

In this study we will discuss some hindrances that obstruct the growth and flow of God's love in our lives. We will also discuss some of the principles that promote and increase the growth of God's love in our lives.

Some of the amazing benefits and results of the **perfect love** of God flowing and working in our lives include: humility, unity, forgiveness, reconciliation of relationships, intensified revival and evangelism, love for our neighbor and enemy and especially the brotherhood (the body of Christ).

Loving God and loving our brother are completely and indivisibly linked, because we are members of one body. Our love for God (the invisible) is manifest by our love for our brother (the visible): *"He who does not love his brother, whom he has seen, cannot love God, whom he has not seen" (1 John 4:20).*

Volume VII
Deeper Life Spiritual Growth Cycle
Relationship, Transformation and Dominion Working in the Love of God

The primary purpose and scope of the lesson series in this book is directed and driven by the greatest need and challenge for the born-again believer in these momentous days of the endtime. And that is to attain the spiritual maturity required to operate in the apostolic power, dominion and authority demonstrated in the book of Acts. Only this course of action will combat and overcome the evil and vicious spirit of the Antichrist rapidly rising in the world today and empower us to effectively reap the end-time harvest.

The seemingly impossible task to reach the lost souls of this godless, hopeless generation, with time running out, sets the stage for God to do a new thing -- a supernatural thing.

Our great omnipotent, omniscient, omnipresent God is calling every born-again believer to partner with Him at the supernatural level as a son of God -- fighting in His battle and working in His harvest with dominion and authority over Satan and sickness:

The key spiritual growth cycle concepts discussed in this book include: Relationship, Transformation and Dominion, all working in the love of God.

Volume VIII
Addendum Volume
PowerPoint Charts for all Volumes

The Addendum Volume contains the 8.5 X 11 copies of the PowerPoint charts supporting the themes and concepts presented in the seven volume series entitled, *"I Must Be About My Father's Business."*

The purpose of these charts is to, the extent possibly, provide a graphic image of a concept as a strawman to initiate and facilitate understanding and discussion of biblical concepts.

The full color charts are available on CD in Adobe Acrobat and PowerPoint formats. For group teaching, these can be printed on printer transparencies for presentation on an overhead projector or with a computer and multi-media projector.

How to purchase copies of these books:

The E-copy of these books can be purchased from web sites: My-Fathers-Business.net (English) and Negocios-De-Me-Padre.net (Spanish). Hard copies and E-copies may be purchased by contacting the author by email: jtwentier@peoplepc.com.

Appendix 3
Notes

Section I

Chapter 1

(1) Webster's New World College Dictionary, Fourth Edition, Copyright © 2002, by Wiley Publishing, Inc., Cleveland Ohio,1598.

(2) *A Look Into Your Heart*, Mt. Carmel and the Prophet Elijah, pamphlet.

Section II

Chapter 1

(1) Author unknown.

(2) Barnes' Notes, Electronic Database, Copyright © 1997, 2003, 2005, 2006 by Biblesoft, Inc. All rights reserved.

Chapter 2

(1) Adam Clarke's Commentary, Electronic Database, Copyright © 1996, 2003, 2005, 2006 by Biblesoft, Inc. All rights reserved.

(2) *Children's Ministry Magazine*, http://childrensministry. com/articles/teaching-kids-to-pray/.

(3) *Prayer Activities for Children,* http://christianity.about. com/od/babydedication /a/SE-Teaching-Children-to-Pray.htm.

Chapter 3

(1) The Pulpit Commentary, Electronic Database, Copyright © 2001, 2003 by Biblesoft, Inc. All rights reserved.

Section III

Chapter 1

(1) Adam Clarke's Commentary, Electronic Database, Copyright © 1996, 2003, 2005, 2006 by Biblesoft, Inc. All rights reserved.

(2) Matthew Henry's Commentary on the whole Bible, PC Study Bible Formatted Electronic Database, Copyright © 2006 by Biblesoft, Inc. All rights reserved.

(3) David K. Bernard, *God's Infallible Word,* (Word Aflame Press, 1992), p. 27, 63-65.

Chapter 2

(1) E. M. Bounds, *E.M. Bounds on Prayer,* (Whitaker House, 1997), p. 11, 12.

(2) Theological Wordbook of the Old Testament. Copyright © 1980 by The Moody Bible Institute of Chicago. All rights reserved. Used by permission.

(3) Barnes' Notes, Electronic Database, Copyright © 1997, 2003, 2005, 2006 by Biblesoft, Inc. All rights reserved.

(4) Author unknown.

Chapter 3

(1) The Pulpit Commentary, Electronic Database, Copyright © 2001, 2003 by Biblesoft, Inc. All rights reserved.

(2) Barnes' Notes, Electronic Database, Copyright © 1997, 2003, 2005, 2006 by Biblesoft, Inc. All rights reserved.

(3) Author unknown.

Chapter 4

(1) Webster's New World College Dictionary, Fourth Edition, Copyright © 2002, by Wiley Publishing, Inc., Cleveland, Ohio,1598.

(2) E. M. Bounds, reference unknown.

(3) Matthew Henry's Commentary on the whole Bible, PC Study Bible Formatted Electronic Database, Copyright © 2006 by Biblesoft, Inc. All rights reserved.

Chapter 5

(1) Jesus' Prayer Request, http://biblebaptistcares.com /2010/10/18 /jesus-prayer-request/.

Appendices

Appendix 7

(1) Don Longworth, *"The Practical Disciple"*, March 23, 2015, "The Forgotten Super-Weapon of the Church", https://fellowshipofaburningheart.wordpress.com/ 2015/03/23/the-forgotten-super-weapon-of-the-church/.

Appendix 4
Misconceptions Regarding Prayer

Below is a brief summary of some misconceptions regarding prayer. There is no intent here to provide a comprehensive list of misconceptions regarding a balanced prayer life. This is simply provided to open the discussion to identify these and other misconceptions that may hinder our pursuit of a more effective and powerful prayer life. A few related Scriptures are provided to give a biblical response.

1. I am so busy I don't have time to pray.

When we give God of our precious resources of time, health (strength) and wealth, etc., He will bless and multiply it.

"If you give, you will receive. Your gift will return to you in full measure, pressed down, shaken together to make room for more, and running over. Whatever measure you use in giving -- large or small -- it will be used to measure what is given back to you "(Luke 6:38). NLT

"But seek ye first the kingdom of God, and his righteousness; and all these things shall be added unto you" (Matt. 6:33, Luke 12:3).

"And Elijah said unto her, Fear not; but make me thereof a little cake first, and after make for thee and for thy son. For thus saith the Lord God of Israel, The barrel of meal shall not waste, neither shall the cruse of oil fail, until the day that the Lord sendeth rain upon the earth. And she went and did according to the saying of Elijah: and she, and he, and her house, did eat many days. And the barrel of meal wasted not, neither did the cruse of oil fail, according to the word of the Lord, which he spake by Elijah" (1 Kings 17:13, 14).

There are numerous examples of prayer and commandments to pray recorded in God's Word (refer to a summary in Appendix 1). While obedience brings blessings to our lives; disobedience will bring curses.

God Blesses Obedience: *"And it shall come to pass, if thou shalt hearken diligently unto the voice of the Lord thy God, to observe and to do all his commandments which I command thee this day, that the Lord thy God will set thee on high above all nations of the earth: And all these blessings shall come on thee, and overtake thee, if thou shalt hearken unto the voice of the Lord thy God. Blessed shalt thou be in the city, and blessed shalt thou be in the field"* (Deut. 28:1-3). Ten verses (4-13) follow, with thirty blessings promised to those who are obedient.

God Curses Disobedience: *"But it shall come to pass, if thou wilt not hearken unto the voice of the Lord thy God, to observe to do all his commandments and his statutes which I command thee this day; that all these curses shall come upon thee, and overtake thee: Cursed shalt thou be in the city, and cursed shalt thou be in the field"* (Deut. 28:15, 16). The next fifty-two verses (17-68) pronounce 117 curses on those who are disobedient.

"Bring ye all the tithes into the storehouse, that there may be meat in mine house, and prove me now herewith, saith the Lord of hosts, if I will not open you the windows of heaven, and pour you out a blessing, that there shall not be room enough to receive it. And I will rebuke the devourer for your sakes, and he shall not destroy the fruits of your ground; neither shall your vine cast her fruit before the time in the field, saith the Lord of hosts" (Mal. 3:10, 11).

This Scripture is generally used to support finances being given to God and the remainder being multiplied. But this also applies to our time which is more valuable than money. When we spend time in prayer, God will multiply our time by making us more productive in our daily tasks and taking problems out of our lives that would save many hours or days of our time.

2. I pray doing chores around the house, driving in my car, etc. vs. setting aside a solitary place to pray.

Although we should have an attitude of prayer as we go about our daily activities (traveling in our car, etc.), is it necessary to have a private place and time of prayer to pray effectual, fervent and balanced prayers. This is addressed in Jesus' instructions to His disciples:

*"But thou, when thou prayest, **enter into thy closet**, and when thou hast shut thy door, pray to thy Father which is in secret; and thy Father which seeth in secret shall reward thee openly. But when ye pray, use not vain repetitions, as the heathen do: for they think that they shall be heard for their much speaking" (Matt. 6:6-15).*

We also see this exampled in the life of Jesus when He often went to a private place alone to pray:

"And when he had sent the multitudes away, he went up into a mountain apart to pray: and when the evening was come, he was there alone" (Matt. 14:23).

"And in the morning, rising up a great while before day, he went out, and departed into a solitary place, and there prayed" (Mark 1:35).

"And when he had sent them away, he departed into a mountain to pray" (Mark 6:46).

"And he withdrew himself into the wilderness, and prayed" (Luke 5:16).

3. Some have made light of prayer seminars and teaching people to pray, saying you should just talk to Jesus like talking to a friend.

The disciples of Jesus asked Him to teach them to pray and He responded to their request. There is great value in training people who are struggling with their daily prayer life, particularly children and new converts. We are very faithful and consistent in teaching them the Word. We should be just as consistent in teaching them the importance and principles of prayer.

"And it came to pass, that, as he was praying in a certain place, when he ceased, one of his disciples said unto him, Lord, teach us to pray, as John also taught his disciples. And he said unto them, When ye pray, say, Our Father which art in heaven, Hallowed be thy name. Thy kingdom come. Thy will be done, as in heaven, so in earth . . ." (Luke 11:1, 2).

4. The statement has been made: "I had rather praise God for ten minutes than to pray for an hour."

Worship and praise are certainly an important part of relationship prayer, but there are other important parts of balanced prayer as described in Sections I and II of this book. Some of these with related Scriptures include:

Relationship prayer (upward focus) – praying for our needs to be supplied:

"Ask, and it shall be given you; seek, and ye shall find; knock, and it shall be opened unto you: For every one that asketh receiveth; and he that seeketh findeth . . ." (Matt. 7:7).

"If ye then, being evil, know how to give good gifts unto your children, how much more shall your Father which is in heaven give good things to them that ask him?" (Matt. 7:11)

"Be careful for nothing; but in every thing by prayer and supplication with thanksgiving let your requests be made known unto God" (Phil. 4:6).

Transformation prayer (inward focus) – praying to be forgiven and changed:

"If my people, which are called by my name, shall humble themselves, and pray, and seek my face, and turn from their wicked ways; then will I hear from heaven, and will forgive their sin, and will heal their land" (2 Chron. 7:14).

"Create in me a clean heart, O God; and renew a right spirit within me. Cast me not away from thy presence; and take not thy holy spirit from me. Restore unto me the joy of thy salvation; and uphold me with thy free spirit. Then will I teach transgressors; and sinners shall be converted" (Psalms 51:10-13).

Dominion prayer (outward focus) – praying for the healing and deliverance of others. Praying for the restoration of apostolic ministry -- the Word confirmed with signs following:

"And he said unto them, This kind can come forth by nothing, but by prayer and fasting" (Mark 9:29).

"Pray ye therefore the Lord of the harvest, that he will send forth labourers into his harvest" (Matt. 9:38).

"Ye have not chosen me, but I have chosen you, and ordained you, that ye should go and bring forth fruit, and that your fruit should remain: that whatsoever ye shall ask of the Father in my name, he may give it you" (John 15:16).

Praying for wisdom to exercise dominion over Satan and sickness in the harvest field and battlefield: *"If any of you lack wisdom, let him ask of God, that giveth to all men liberally, and upbraideth not; and it shall be given him" (James 1:5).*

Praying like Daniel who was repenting for the nation of Israel and praying for the fulfillment of the prophesied restoration to their homeland: *"And I set my face unto the Lord God, to seek by prayer and supplication, with fasting, and sackcloth, and ashes: And I prayed unto the Lord my God, and made my confession, and said, O Lord, the great and dreadful God, keeping the covenant and mercy to them that love him, and to them that keep his commandments; O my God, incline thine ear, and hear; open thine eyes, and behold our desolations, and the city which is called by thy name: for we do not present our supplications before thee for our righteousnesses, but for thy great mercies" (Dan. 9:3, 4, 18).*

5. After a few minutes, I run out of things to say and how to pray.

The purpose of this book is to address this very valid concern expressed by a significant portion of the laity:

(1) Identifying the basic, simple components of prayer focused on our upward relationship with God, our inward need to be transformed and our outward reach to those in need. This provides an outline for one to use their own words in expressing their heart to God.

(2) Identifying the importance and need emphasized in Scripture for praying in the Spirit as well as praying with the understanding. When words fail us, the Spirit knows what to say and how to pray on our behalf.

(3) Identifying the value of prayer teams built around common needs.

(4) Providing sample prayer agendas to assist in focused prayer. The words should be changed to fit each unique situation.

Appendix 5
Prayer Ministry Tools

The following are two examples of tools that can be used to highlight the importance of prayer and assist in increasing the amount of balanced and effective prayer going on in the church. These may be used in conjunction with a prayer seminar, or a time of special teaching on prayer.

5.1 Anonymous and Confidential Prayer Survey

The purpose of this sample survey (Exhibit 1 on the following page) is to:

(a) Measure how much total prayer is being offered up each week by the church.

(b) Identify any problems or issues that should be addressed to help people pray more effective prayers.

(c) Identify the need for teaching on focused and effective prayer.

(d) Capture a baseline to measure how much improvement is made in the total prayer effort of the church over the following months.

Appendices

5.2 Faith Promise Prayer Pledge and Offering Cards

These prayer pledge and offering cards may be used in the prayer ministry of the church to bring greater emphasis to prayer and the need to increase the amount of prayer being offered up in the church. We often do this to solicit finances for various church projects or missions giving. It has been said: "You get what you measure and you measure what is important."

Exhibit 2 on the following page is a sample of: a **Faith Promise Prayer Pledge Card** and a **Faith Promise Prayer Offering Card,** both of which would be submitted anomalously, without the individual's name. The pledge card would be used to make a prayer commitment for 3, 6 or 12 months, etc.

The prayer offering card would be used each week or month, for a period of time, to indicate the amount of time spent in prayer by the church members. The total number of hours being prayed and pledged would be displayed in the church in a prominent location.

These exhibits are samples and should be changed to fit the unique needs of each church.

Exhibit 1

Anonymous and Confidential Prayer Survey
Do not put your name on this survey

1. _____ Hours of prayer prayed each week (not including regular church services).

   _____ Percent of time praying for you and your family's needs.

   _____ Percent of time praying for others (including lost souls).

2. With your busy schedule do you often find you don't have time to pray?   No: ___ Yes: ___

3. Do you find it difficult to pray in the Spirit (praying in tongues) on a regular basis?   No ___ Yes ___

4. Do you have difficulty praying for 30 - 60 minutes because you run out of things to say or don't know how to pray?

   No: ___ Yes: ___

5. Do you think teaching on different types of prayer (relationship, transformation and dominion prayer) would help you to be more effective in praying focused prayers?   No: ___ Yes: ___

6. Do you think participating in a small group prayer meeting with a prayer leader leading in focused prayer would help you learn to pray more effectively?   No: ___ Yes: ___

7. Do you a have a guilt feeling regarding your struggle or frustration with prayer? Occasionally: _____ Often: _____

Comments or Suggestions:

Faith Promise Prayer Pledge:

Today's Date: _____

By faith I pledge a sacrifice offering of prayer:

Hours of Prayer Each Week: _____

For the next: ___ 3 months ___ 6 months or ___ months

"The effectual fervent prayer of a righteous man availeth much"

"This kind can come forth by nothing, but by prayer and fasting"

Faith Promise Prayer Offering:

Today's Date: _____

Check One: For the Week ____ or, for the Month ____

My sacrifice offering of Prayer: _____ (Hours)

"The effectual fervent prayer of a righteous man availeth much"

"This kind can come forth by nothing, but by prayer and fasting"

Appendix 6
Parenting and Prayer Notes

This chapter provides a few snapshots of time in the journey of guiding my two children through the stages of life from childhood to adulthood. This is provided for parents to help them recognize the fleeting opportunities that are available to them during small windows of time in their child's life, particularly in teaching them to pray. The following pages are some of my unedited writings that reflect my emotions and concerns regarding my responsibilities as a parent to guide them, particularly as it related to their spiritual welfare and prayer.

I include these to point out that I was well aware of the responsibilities and important issues in raising children; and I did many things well. And although my grown children are doing good and living successful lives, I do have one regret that continues to trouble me today. And that is, I wish I had understood more about prayer and the process of teaching my children to pray, particularly during their formative years. I wish I had known the basic principles of prayer presented in this book.

I trust that, at the risk of being too transparent, the following will cause you to pause and identify every window of opportunity to teach and influence your children for righteousness -- particularly through the avenue of prayer (your prayers and teaching them to pray). And that when looking back in time, after your parenting process is recorded in the pages of history, you will have no regrets.

Appendices

	Date	To	Description
1	1987	My wife	My concerns regarding parenting opportunities and responsibilities for our two children (11 and 12).
2	2000	Misty	My words at my daughter's wedding.
3	2002	Monte	Letter to my son a few days prior to his wedding.
4	2006	Misty, Tim, Monte, Starla	Letter to my grown children and their spouses several years after they had been married, regarding living a successful spiritual and physical life.

Attachment 1
Concerns regarding our children at ages 11 and 12

September 1987

Regarding Misty and Monte:

Two beautiful children have been given to us to love, train and mold into beautiful, respectful, successful and happy teenagers and young adults.

Our direct influence in this process is already half over, considering that at the age of 18-20 they will be or will be becoming independent (Misty 12/18 = 66%; Monte 11/18 = 61%). Each year that has passed and will pass after their 6th birthday, we have had and will have less and less direct influence on the direction and outcome of their lives.

In just 1 year Missy will be a teenager, in 6 years she will be 18. In 2 years Bubba will be a teenager and in 7 years he will be 18. The next 6 or 7 years will fly by much faster than the ones since they were just toddlers. Therefore, the things that are important to us as parents and the things that we know are needed to make them happy and successful Christians and citizens, must have been imparted to them yesterday and in the now timeframe.

To say it another way, we are at a very critical juncture (pre-teen) in their lives. A casual attitude and approach on our part, in pursuing the things that we know are best for them, will have permanent consequences that may adversely affect their future (which is also our future).

The future and success of Missy and Bubba is more important to me than anything else in this life. It is on the very top of my priority list, although I have not always given it my best attention.

253

Mother nature and the home environment dictates that the mother probably has more than 50% of the influence in this process of raising children, particularly since she has the opportunity to be with them more as well as many other reasons.

That does not mean that I can relegate the whole responsibility to you, but hopefully you will think seriously about these things and join with me in a more dedicated approach to leading, guiding and teaching them the right things; the right way; at the right time.

I plan to develop a list of current and future goals and objectives, for both Misty and Monte that is reasonable and safe for them to reach for as they progress in their development from childhood to adults. I will also develop a plan which outlines the things that we and they must do to make our dream for them come true. These plans will need to be revisited and changed from time to time as we move further down life's road and can see more clearly the things that lie ahead.

Just writing these things down will not make it happen, but it will serve to remind us of some of the obligations and opportunities that we have now, to do some positive things. These opportunities will often be available for only a thin slice of time, and unless we are alert and ready, we will miss them and see them only after they have passed. So let's make the most of these golden opportunities, as we experience the transition of our relationship with our children change from the role of a parent to the role of a friend, over the next few years.

Just writing these few short words has helped me put some of these things in a better perspective and made me realize the importance of setting goals and making plans to see them happen. And, the lump in my throat and the mist in my eye reaffirm to me that these reflections are more than just words, they are my feelings.

Their Dad

Attachment 2
Dad's words at Misty's wedding

December 2, 2000

The year was 1967 the date was December 2nd, 33 years ago tonight, that your mother and I were married by pastor Kilgore. It was at the original Life Tabernacle location on Market and Rouse.

So tonight, we are celebrating together with you and Tim.

Happy anniversary to my dear wife, and congratulations to you and Tim on your wedding night.

The year was 1975; the date was May 29th; the hour was 6am in the morning, and I was presented with a 6 lb. 9 oz., beautiful, miracle gift from God and your mother.

I was shaken and shocked at the perfection and love of a beautiful newborn baby girl. You were a happy, and perfect baby in every way. We woke you up to feed you and play with you. And since you never cried, we thought we really had the parenting routine down, with the wisdom of our late years.

But God humbled us less than 15 months later, when He sent us another beautiful gift – your brother - a 9 lb. 12 oz. kicking, hungry, and screaming baby boy. It was then that I wanted to find that old-time preacher that had prayed that your mother could have a child, so I could tell him to stop praying, and to please cancel the request for more miracles.

I have watched now for 25 years, 180 days, 12 hours, and 33 minutes as the miracle of beauty and love has unfolded in our home and in our lives. And I stand here in awe and shock again tonight looking at an even more perfect and beautiful gift.

I want to publicly affirm you and publicly say, "that you have met and exceeded all of my expectations as a daughter". The term we use in the business world would be, "significantly exceeds all expectations".

I just want to encourage and challenge you and Tim to continue on in your relationship with God and reach your potential, working in His Kingdom. Because that is where you will find true fulfillment and happiness in life.

For the past 25½ years, it has been a wonderful trip, a quick trip. And looking back, I have no regrets. We have brought you to this wonderful church, that has been in the center of our lives, every time the doors were opened. And we have watched, as God has touched you and changed your life at the altar of consecration.

We have had so many good family devotions in our home, with Bible study and prayers together. We have spent so many wonderful times together, a lot of laugher, and only a few tears.

And I want to remind you that it is not only our family's love for God and the church, that has brought the blessings of God into your life, but also the godly heritage of past generations on both sides of your family.

I know you have taken so long to find a companion, because you were looking for someone like your dad. Well, you tried and you have done very good. And there are a few similarities: he is good-looking, he knows a little about software and computers, but best of all he loves God, and he loves you, and that really is my only requirement.

I remember when you started driving. It was a hard adjustment for me to turn you lose in Houston traffic — particularly after you totaled out one of my cars. During those mid-teens to early 20 years, I sometimes struggled with the 3 "c's" — and that was cash, cars and college, and now tonight cash again. But I was glad to make the investment, and you have made every dollar worth it, many times over. You have been a great and joyful return on our investment.

I do want to remind you that you owe us one sometime in the future. Not in dollars and cents (although we won't turn that down either), but in giving us another little Misty miracle. That will help us remember and relive the best and happiest day of our lives, as your mom and dad.

And then you will begin to understand our love for you, when you are holding one of your own.

Oh, my dear, sweet Misty, where have all the years gone, how did you grow up so fast. I tried to slow it down, but time just kept moving.

It seems like only yesterday that I was standing at the altar with you in my arms for your dedication. And now we are at the altar once again for another wonderful and special occasion.

It has been such a wonderful trip, a great ride. And I want to thank our great God tonight for the wonderful years, the wonderful times. It is all because of Him and His love, that we have experienced so much love for so many years in our family and in our church.

And tonight, we are writing the final lines of one chapter of our lives. And as we do, we can't help but look back and remember the wonderful things in the past and the blessings of God in it all.

But life is forever moving and forever unfolding. And tonight, we are beginning a new chapter of life. A chapter in which the love in our family will expand and make room for a new member, a new son.

One of the greatest joys of being your father was to see the bond of love between you and your brother as closest and best of friends.

Maybe once in a 100 years there is a double bond between a girl and her father and a girl and her brother like we have had in our home. It is something special. And it cannot be explained or described. It can only be observed and felt.

And I thank God that Monte and I have been a part of that, a special bond of love between both of us and you. I guess you can sum it up by saying, the ones who know you the most, admire and love you the most.

You are blessed tonight as the most loved and admired lady in the world by the men in your life. And you have been blessed thrice -- thrice blessed.

Because now there are three:

1. Now there is Timmy,
   2. And then there is Monte,
      3. And there has always been, and there will always be me.

Your Dad

Attachment 3
A letter to my son before his wedding

November 2002

Monte, My dear son and best friend,

It is late Sunday night and I am sitting in my office remembering a lot of good things that have happened over the past 26 years since you were born. And I am thinking about you and all the good years we have enjoyed you in our home and in our lives. And I am thinking that there is not another boy in the world that has been more loved than you have been loved by a mom and dad.

Your mom and I have done everything we knew to do to give you every advantage in life to be successful in your Christian walk, in your education, in your career, in your finances and in your social life with family and good friends.

And yet I sit here wondering was there something else I could have done more to have helped you more as a father, as a teacher, as an example, and as the spiritual leader of our home. Looking back I now see two things I should have done better to help you with your daily personal devotion with God, and I pray there will be opportunity for me to make up for that in the future.

(1) Teaching you to pray. I prayed with you and for you a lot and set the example of prayer in our home, but I should have helped you more with your daily prayer life.

(2) Teaching you how to study God's Word. We had family devotions with Bible lessons and I tried to teach you many things, but I should have helped you more to learn how to go beyond reading the Bible to studying the Bible.

I have always prayed that if there was a failure on my part that affected you in a negative way, that God would punish me and spare you.

So, with these thoughts in mind I felt I needed to say a few things to you from my heart as you begin a new chapter in your life with a beautiful and godly companion that we have prayed for and God has given to you and to us.

Your mother and I have prayed and fasted for you all of your life. And we are now on a few days of fasting and prayer and a part of the purpose for that is for you and Starla as you begin your life together.

The following is a list of some of the things we have prayed for you all your life, and we have already seen God answer many of them.

- That you would find God's will for your life and have a close personal relationship with God.

- That you would remember and honor the heritage of truth and faith handed down to you by your parents and grandparents and your wonderful pastors. And that when the time came you would be diligent to teach it to your children so that they would have the same chance to be saved that you had.

- That you would come to realize early in life that Jesus Christ is the only source and meaning of peace and happiness in life and to put Him first in your life.

- That you would learn to trust God and depend on Him in times of difficulty and trial.

- That you would find the right lifelong companion that would love God first in their life, and love you, and love us and be like another daughter in our family. And until then you would keep yourself pure.

- That you would find the right job and career. A job that will allow you to make a good living but not interfere with faithfulness to God's house and God's work.

- We have prayed every day of your life that you would be:

> - Protected from the evils and temptations of this world,
>   - Protected from sickness and disease,
>   - Protected from harm and danger.

  - We have prayed that you would always put God first in your life and have a close personal relationship with Him that only comes with a daily devotion of prayer and His Word.

As you begin this new chapter in life and a new responsibility in your life as the head of your home and as the spiritual leader of your home, I want to recount a few foundational things that I have tried to practice in my life and in our home, that has made our marriage and home successful and secure:

1. Seek first the Kingdom of God and all the other things will be added to you. Put God first in your finances and time.

2. Be as faithful to God's house as you are to your job. I never missed work. I went to work feeling bad and sometimes sick. I made a decision one time and for all times a long time ago that we would be in the house of God every time the doors are open. The question was never asked in our home: "Are we going to church tonight?" When I had to work late, I had some extra clothes in my car and shaved in the parking lot. And our family has benefited from this decision over and over again.

3. Be honest in everything even when it cost you money or hurts you in other ways. There will be times when it will cost you to be honest on your income taxes to report cash income, etc. But God will make up the difference 10 times over when we follow the principles and laws in His Word. His blessings will be withheld when we violate or go against any of His laws.

4. Always have people in your life and around you that will influence you and challenge you and help you to be better.

5. Always have someone in your life that you can help in some way, that you can lift up and encourage.

261

Appendices

6. Be a good influence on those in your circle of influence. Help pull them up and lift them up rather than them pulling you down to their level. Being a godly man is more than just for yourself, because your wife and others watching your life will be affected. You have a gift from God and the potential to be a leader, but remember a leader must be a step ahead of the others and always behind God following Him and His ways.

7. Remember that every decision you make now not only affects you, but it will also affect your wife and in the future your children. I have had to make some unselfish decisions in my life, decisions that was not what was best for me, but what was best for my family.

8. Last and most important, lift your wife up spiritually and let her lift you up. She will have some strengths where you may not be as strong, and you will have some strengths where she may not be as strong. Combine your strengths and not your weaknesses. Don't let one of your strengths be cancelled out by the other's weakness. And don't let anything you do pull the other one down.

When there is any issue that affects spiritual decisions in your home, where you each have a different opinion, take the one with the higher standard where your home can be pulled up to the higher level rather than being pulled down to the lower level.

Always let the altar and the Bible and the church and your love for God and your family be in the center of your life and not the entertainment center. Establish a daily devotion time in your life with prayer and studying the Word of God. If this is not done, the touch of God you get on Sunday night will be lost by the next week and you will not make good progress as a Christian. It is a daily walk. If you feed the carnal man he will rule your life. If you feed the spiritual man he will be dominant in your life and your family will experience the rich and lasting benefits.

3 John 2-4
2 I wish above all things that thou mayest prosper and be in health, even as thy soul prospereth.
3 For I rejoiced greatly, when the brethren came and testified of the truth that is in thee, even as thou walkest in the truth.
4 I have no greater joy than to hear that my children walk in truth.

Never forget who you are:

- *You are God's child, you have been born again of the water and Spirit. We dedicated you to Him and gave you back to Him in September of 1976. I just listened to the dedication tape this week.*

- *You are a son of God, seek to please Him and have His favor.*

- *You are your father's and mother's son. You have a godly heritage of parents, and grandparents on both sides of your family and Starla does also.*

- *You are made of good stuff – tough stuff. Keep walking in God's ways. Keep walking in our footsteps.*

Your mom and I have always prayed that whatever it takes that you would be saved and meet us in heaven. And now we include your beautiful wife Starla in that prayer.

And if anything ever happens to me and I don't have the opportunity to say good-bye at the end of my life, like our good friend Ray Plant, who was suddenly taken from us, let me say it now:

"Be there! No matter what it takes, be there!
Meet me there! Meet me in heaven.
I will be waiting for you there -- just inside the Eastern Gate."

Monte, you are the pride and joy of my life and I love you more than you will ever know.

Dad

Appendices

Attachment 4
Letter to my children and their spouses several years after they had been married.

April 27, 2006

To: Misty and Tim, Monte and Starla

This book is a place to put some of my notes and messages to you from the past, the present and the future. Many of the things that I will share with you are things God has talked to me about and I have shared with others in the classroom and in the pulpit.

I know I walk a thin and difficult line between fulfilling my responsibility as the leader of our family (not your home) and not over-reaching or over-stepping in this area. There is not a clear-cut definition to guide me in this area, but I know that in some way I still have some overarching responsibilities for our family. You probably will not understand this until your children are grown and on their own and you are grandparents.

Your mom and I carry a burden for you and pray for you every day. We took one day this week to specifically fast and pray for you. When you are going through difficulties we will be burdened with you and when you are experiencing good times, we will rejoice with you.

I am very thankful and happy that you have your own home and family and I recognize and respect that the decisions that I once made for you are now in your hands. I also recognize that the only positive role your mom and I can now play in your life is one of influence and example. The amount of influence we now have in your life is directly related to the depth of relationship that we built with you during the wonderful and precious few years we had you as an infant, a child, a teenager and a young adult living in our home. And I trust that our relationship bridge is strong and that it can be described today and in the future as best friends.

I don't know if it is good news or bad news, but as long as I am alive, I will never quit communicating -- talking to you, writing to you, encouraging you and praying for you regarding the important and eternal issues of life. And when I am gone, I pray that I will leave a godly heritage of example and influence that will guide and help you on your road to heaven.

P.S.
Over the past 64 years I have figured out the important things in life. Two of these important things that make a successful life are listed below and are a lot of what this collection of documents is all about:

- The big "C" Communication: Talking to God; God talking to us and good communication with our family and friends.

- The big "D" Discipline: The only process that will align what we are doing with what we should be doing.

Appendix 7
Children's Prayer: The Forgotten Super Weapon of the Church [1]

I've been on a personal journey of discovering the incredible power of prayer. For most of my life though, prayer seemed ridiculously boring, powerless and mundane. I grew up in the church; the son of missionaries. Prayer meetings were by far the most boring thing I ever endured. By the time I was a teenager, I had logged hundreds and hundreds of hours in prayer meetings. Mind you, it was hundreds of hours of fidgeting, dozing, staring at the ceiling and poking my sister for entertainment while the adults droned on and on. Many prayers were earnest and I could tell these people were touching God. Most prayers though, were fluffy, long winded and full of big words. Prayer meetings were absolutely mind-numbing.

The reason I'm pondering this, is because I don't want my children to grow up with the same distaste for prayer. I want to empower them with it early on. As I look back, I think it would have helped to have a true spirit-filled prayer warrior take us youngsters under his/her wing and teach us to pray with faith and power that shakes hell. It would have been amazing to pray with other earnest young people and experience specific answers to prayer together. Children have great faith and this is an enormously powerful weapon that the church has not tapped.

During my time in rural West Africa, I observed 4-5 year old children driving large herds of cattle with their older brothers. I observed girls of the same age bring water home from the wells. Even the youngest kids were proud to bring solid contributions to their families. If they got sick, or could not perform their responsibilities the whole family felt their absence.

All this even filtered down to our candle-lit evening prayer meetings in the villages. Children prayed without hesitation alongside adults. The leader would assign prayer requests to adults and children alike. An adult's prayer request would be given to a child and a child's prayer request would be given to an adult to pray. It was beautiful!

Kids take pride in being needed, it helps them grow up with confidence. Giving kids responsibility is one of the lost things in our society. We have stripped children of it in the North American church. They bring indispensable contributions to the family and church. Sitting in chairs, learning to be quiet and respectful are important skills, but we have unconsciously taught them to stay "spiritual consumers" within the church without really contributing or being expected to contribute. The extent of their involvement is usually at Christmas and Easter when they get up and reluctantly entertain the church with a song or two. Hmm, I wonder why it's hard to engage them when they're older?

Imagine, though for a moment, if the mighty faith of children were employed to pray a sinner through to conversion? Imagine what that would do for their faith? Imagine what that would do for the church? The power of their faith is untapped and indispensable.

I've read of children in China, praying over the sick and seeing miraculous and instantaneous healing: "The Heavenly Man" by Brother Yun.

Previous to the 1970 revival in Saskatoon, Bill McLeod

organized children's prayer meetings to run concurrently with the adult prayer meeting. He didn't just send the kids downstairs for another lesson or to be entertained. Adults supervised and coached them how to pray with power and the kids would lead their own prayer meetings. They learned the power of prayer and confidence.

The great Moravian revival that sparked the first modern missionary movement was hugely influenced by the prayer of children and a 24/7 prayer meeting that never ceased for over 100 years began: Here is a quote from Tony Cauchi's article on the Moravian revival on Revival-Library.org.

> *"A few days after the 13th of August, a remarkable revival took place among the children at Herrnhut and Bertholdsdorf. On the 18th of August, all the children at the boarding school were seized with an extraordinary impulse of the Spirit, and spent the whole night in prayer. From this time, a constant work of God was going on in the minds of the children, in both places. No words can express the powerful operation of the Holy Spirit upon these children, whose lives were so transformed.*
>
> *On the 25th of August, the brethren began the ministry of 24 hour-a-day prayer which continued for over a hundred years. They considered that, as in the ancient Temple the fire on the altar never ceased to burn, so in the Church, which is now the Temple of God, the prayers of the saints ought always to ascend to the Lord."*

Jesus wasn't kidding that "the Kingdom of God belongs to such as these." Let's stop sidelining our kids, especially when it comes to prayer. The next revival may swing on their mighty prayers of faith.

Appendix 8
About the Author

The author's background includes three different areas of experience:

(1) Working thirty-three years in the challenging and exciting field of computer technology, serving both as a technologist and a manager, witnessing and experiencing almost unbelievable accomplishments and advancements.

(2) Working 50 years in various ministries in three home churches, serving at the individual and leadership levels: Home Bible Study and Discipleship Ministry (40 years), Sunday School Bus Ministry (10) Years, Sunday School Ministry, Compassion and Care Ministry, Home Fellowship Ministry, Youth Ministry, Visitor Follow-up Ministry, Nursing Home Ministry, Singles Ministry, Alcohol / Drug Abuse Mentoring Ministry and Prison Ministry.

(3) Preaching and teaching in many churches in the U.S., foreign missions churches and Bible schools (primarily as a revivalist vs. an evangelist).

His ministry emphasis includes revival and spiritual growth of the saint for the purpose of more effective evangelism of a lost world. Some of the key ministry themes include:

- Relationship with God (impartation from the Father).
- Spiritual Growth (continuous transformation).
- Dominion (engagement in the Father's business with dominion over satan and sickness).
- God's perfect love growing and flowing in our lives.
- Urgency of the Father's business (managing our priorities consistent with our knowledge of the times).

If you want to contact James Twentier, or would like more information about this ministry, please do so by one of the following methods:

Telephone: (281) 773-6534

Email: jtwentier@peoplepc.com

Websites: My-Fathers-Business.net (English)

Negocios-De-Me-Padre.net (Español)

Ministry Projects:

Foreign Missions (particularly Bible schools)
We have spent several months teaching in Bible schools in: Manila, Philippines; Barcelona, Spain; and Madrid, Spain. We plan to continue this ministry in the future.

Home Missions
(Pioneer works and small churches where the pastor has to work)

Every year a portion of our time is dedicated to this area. This is done on a volunteer basis with no expense to the pastor or the church.

Established Churches

The primary purpose is to encourage and equip the church to develop a better defined and stronger Prayer Ministry (power arm of the church) and Care Ministry (actions arm of the church).

Ministry Focus

Our primary ministry is as a revivalist vs. an evangelist. Our ministry focus is **revival for the saints** which is designed to encourage and equip them to achieve a more effective and disciplined level of spiritual growth and personal evangelism.

Special Services and Seminars

When needed, special services and seminars provide teaching and training for putting practical revival and evangelism principles into practice through the two arms of the church:

- The **Power Arm** (Prayer Ministry --reaching for Him).
- The **Actions Arm** (Compassion and Care Ministry -- reaching for them).

Ministry Information

Some of these services and seminars apply to the entire church and some to selected groups in the church. Multimedia is used in the teaching and training presentations.

- **Outreach Vision and Planning** *(Direction)*
  - Planning for a great Harvest and planning to retain the Harvest.
  - Conducting a Vision and Outreach Planning Session (weekend retreat, or planning meetings).

- **Prayer Ministry** *(Power)*
  - Planning and developing a more powerful Prayer Ministry in the church.
  - Developing a greater understanding and commitment to revival prayer *(Revival Prayer vs. Survival Prayer)*.

- **Compassion and Care Ministry** *(Actions)*
  - Attracting, Winning, Retaining and making Disciples.
  - Reaching sinners in our circle of influence.
  - Caring for visitors and new converts.
    Find a need and fill it !   Find a Hurt and heal it !

- **Team Building and Training** *(Teams)*
  - Developing a better understanding of how to be more effective with ministry teams.
  - Teamwork (unity) makes the dream work (vision)!

V021617-v1